THE 'PEANUT BUTTER' Cookbook

OTHER BOOKS BY WILLIAM I. KAUFMAN

THE NUT COOKBOOK

THE COFFEE COOKBOOK

THE WONDERFUL WORLD OF COOKING SERIES:

Near East-Far East

Caribbean-Latin American

Northern European

Southern European

THE SUGAR FREE COOKBOOK

THE ART OF INDIA'S COOKERY

THE ART OF CREOLE COOKERY

COOKING WITH THE EXPERTS

THE THOS. COOK & SON POCKET TRAVEL GUIDES:

Cook's Pocket Travel Guide to Europe

Cook's Pocket Travel Guide to the West Indies

IT PAYS TO FINISH HIGH SCHOOL

YOUR CAREER IN TELEVISION

BEST TELEVISION PLAYS VOLUMES I, II, III, IV

HOW TO WRITE FOR TELEVISION

HOW TO DIRECT FOR TELEVISION

HOW TO ANNOUNCE FOR TELEVISION

HOW TO WRITE AND DIRECT FOR TELEVISION

The 'I LOVE PEANUT BUTTER' Cookbook

William I. Kaufman

BART

NEW YORK

Reprinted by arrangement with the author

ISBN: 1-55785-026-7

First Bart Books edition: 1988

Bart Books
155 E. 34th Street
New York, New York 10016

Manufactured in the United States of America

THE 'I LOVE PEANUT BUTTER' COOKBOOK

is dedicated to
Tom & Bobbie
for projecting their
peanut butter
enthusiasm
to me.

ACKNOWLEDGMENT

I want to thank the Peanut Growers of Alabama and Georgia for making available their complete kitchen testing facilities and all records and files pertaining to the various phases of peanuts and peanut butter. The National Peanut Council has also extended invaluable assistance to me in this project.

INTRODUCTION

From the time of childhood most Americans think of peanut butter as a basic food for sandwiches and spreads. It is my wish to change this thought.

Peanut butter isn't only for sandwiches. And peanut butter isn't *only* the wholesome, reliable stand-by when the pantry is bare of elaborate foods. Plain as it is, peanut butter can be very fancy indeed.

In Africa and the East, both Near and Far, peanuts and peanut butter are an important part of the cooking. They're used in sauces, stews, bread, and garnishes. In South America, where the peanut first grew, peanut butter is often mixed with honey or cocoa as a spread. And for centuries, Latin Americans have known the zest that peanut butter can give to meat and poultry.

For the imaginative cook, peanut butter is one of the most nutritious, flexible, and economical foods available. Virtually no other food ranks so high in such a wide range of nutritive elements necessary to maintain health in both adults and children.

Peanut butter is as versatile as it is nutritionally virtuous. Here are just some of the ways it can be used:

. . . As a *spread* for crackers or sandwiches, peanut butter combines compatibly with almost any food you could name: jam and jelly, fruit (banana slices, for example), vegetables (green pepper rings), meat, and cheese.

. . . As a *dip*, for such things as potato chips, peanut butter gives added interest to deviled ham, sour cream, and a number of other food specialties.

. . . As a *flavoring agent*, peanut butter knows few limits. It adds texture and flavor to sauces for meat, fish, and poultry. It gives a special smoothness and taste to baked products—biscuits, muffins, pies, cakes, cookies. It's delicious in pudding and ice cream. And that tantalizing "something extra" in a soup or a salad dressing.

Reach for the jar of peanut butter. But when you reach for it, don't be confused by the fact that different brands have different words to describe the peanut butter on the label. Creamy, smooth, creme smooth, creamy blend or similar statements all mean that the peanut butter is as smooth as can be made. If the jar is labeled crunchy, crunch or chunk style, to name a few descriptions, that indicates that the fine pieces of peanut have deliberately been included in the peanut butter to add texture. In some cases, the recipes indicate which type of peanut butter is best; in other cases, the recipes say only "peanut butter." In the latter, either kind may be used with equal success.

Bring new dash to everyday meals and a delightful touch to party dishes. I LOVE PEANUT BUTTER! and I hope you do too.

Table of Contents

PEANUT BUTTER FROM
THE VINE TO THE JAR

Peanut butter is regarded as the all-American food for good reason. It is native to America, although not to the United States. Excavations of Inca tombs in Peru have revealed that the peanut was native to that region and was eaten long before Columbus discovered America.

It was the European explorers following Columbus, though, who introduced the peanut to the rest of the world.

According to records of the early sixteenth century, the peanut was probably imported into Africa and India by the Portuguese traders and into Spain and the Far East by the Spaniards. By this circuitous route, many authorities believe, the peanut returned to the Americas again in the eighteenth and nineteenth centuries, this time carried to North America on the ships transporting slaves. Primarily intended as food for the slaves during the long ocean crossing, the peanuts that were left over from these voyages were planted around the doorsteps of the slave cabins. This was the beginning of what was to become one of the most important crops in the United States.

Peanuts are raised chiefly in the parts of the United States where there is a long growing season and adequate soil and rainfall. Almost half of the peanuts grown in the United States are grown in the Georgia-Alabama and Northern Florida region.

Other important implantations are to be found in the Virginia-Carolina area and the Texas-Oklahoma area.

The peanut is a legume, similar to the pea and the bean. Thomas Jefferson called peanuts "ground peas," and in most foreign countries they are referred to as "groundnuts." It is easy to understand how the peanut got these names, because the plant, when growing, resembles a pea vine with light green leaves. The American varieties are called either "bunch types," because they grow from a center stem in an upright manner, or "runner types," because the stem trails along the ground like a vine. Beautiful small yellow-to-orange flowers form at the joints of the peanut plant where the leaves are attached to the stem. A shoot, or "peg," develops as the flower withers. This shoot continues to grow in the direction of the ground until it pushes its tip into the earth, where the pea pod forms. Light, well-drained soil that does not pack or harden from the rain and sun is needed to allow the peg to enter the ground. When fully grown the peanut shell contains one to three nuts. At harvesting the peanuts are exposed by digging or plowing. They are then trucked to a shelling plant to be cleaned and shelled, screened and sorted according to size and quality before being diverted to packing and to peanut butter manufacturing.

Peanut butter was invented by a doctor in St. Louis in 1890 during his search for a high-protein food for his patients. He ground up roasted peanuts in a meat grinder, added salt, and fed it to his patients as an easily digested, high-protein food.

The new "health food" was immediately successful. It wasn't long before the grocer sold it to his customer from large tubs or pails. It was customary for him to take a large wooden paddle and stir the peanut butter so that its consistency would be uniform before he dipped it up to be carried out. Soon this new food became recognized by many people besides those interested in its high protein. Many bought it only for its delicious taste. A new industry grew up. Today, through the efforts of scientific research, the stabilization process (which keeps the peanuts and the peanut oils from separating) affords us the possibility of enjoying a peanut butter that is creamy and smooth or one that is crunchy. Each nut used in these processes is cleaned again when it reaches the peanut butter plant. Then it is roasted, divested of its skin, and blanched before being subjected to the large grinding mills used in the final step of manufacturing. Each brand has its own manufacturing techniques, which are closely guarded trade secrets.

Peanut butter is one of the most nutritious foods known to man. The United States Department of Agriculture rates peanut butter near the top in six nutritional categories: energy, protein, fat, phosphorus, niacin, and thiamine. Americans are availing themselves of this nutritional bargain by consuming more than 231,000 tons of peanut butter each year. Four out of every five American homes have a kitchen shelf containing a jar of peanut butter. You can put this staple to imaginative uses with THE 'I LOVE PEANUT BUTTER' COOKBOOK.

—*William I. Kaufman*

Appetizers

PÂTÉ, SOUTHERN STYLE

8 ounces raw chicken
  livers
¼ cup smooth peanut
  butter
2 tablespoons cognac
2 tablespoons liquid
  from chicken livers

¾ teaspoon salt
¼ teaspoon nutmeg
1 teaspoon dry mustard
1 tablespoon grated onion
Dash of hot pepper sauce
¼ cup finely chopped
  stuffed olives

To each ¼ cup smooth or crunchy peanut butter add enough water to just cover livers. Cover with lid and simmer 15 minutes. Drain, reserving 2 tablespoons of liquid.

Put livers through sieve or finest blade of grinder. Mix with remaining ingredients, blending thoroughly.

Pack into container, cover, and store in refrigerator until well chilled. Serve with thin toast.

Yield: 1¾ cups

CELERY STUFFED WITH
PEANUT BUTTER HORSE-RADISH

To each ¼ cup smooth or crunchy peanut butter add 1 tablespoon horse-radish. If necessary, add a small amount of water to soften mixture. Allow about 1 tablespoon peanut butter mixture for each stalk of celery and spread into hollow of the celery stalk. Wrap stuffed celery stalks in transparent plastic or aluminum foil to chill.

ALABAMA PEANUT BUTTER STICKS

9 slices day-old white
  bread
1 cup smooth peanut
  butter

½ teaspoon salt
½ cup peanut oil

Trim crusts from bread slices and cut each slice into 5 finger-length pieces. Toast bread and crusts in a slow (250°) oven about 30 minutes or until crisp. Roll crusts to make crumbs (about 1½ cups are needed).

Mix peanut butter with salt and oil.

Dip crisped bread sticks in peanut butter mixture and then roll in bread crumbs. Let dry on paper towels. Serve as snack or with soup. Makes about 45 sticks.

Variation: Add 2 teaspoons grated onion, 4 teaspoons horse-radish, 2 teaspoons Worcestershire sauce and an additional ⅓ cup peanut oil to peanut mixture.

PEANUT BUTTER HAM SQUARES

½ cup peanut butter
2 teaspoons grated onion
6 thin slices boiled ham
1 egg, beaten

2 tablespoons water
½ cup fine, dry bread
  crumbs
1 cup peanut oil

Mix peanut butter and onion. Spread mixture on half the ham slices. Top with remaining ham slices. Wrap in waxed paper and chill in refrigerator for about an hour. Cut into 1-inch squares.

Mix beaten egg with water. Dip squares in egg and then in bread crumbs. Fry in hot peanut oil about 2 minutes or until golden brown. Serve at once on toothpicks.

Yield: 5 dozen canapés

DEVILED PEANUT SPREAD

½ cup peanut butter
1 2¼-ounce can deviled ham
½ teaspoon celery salt

Mix all ingredients lightly. Serve as spread on crackers.

Yield: ⅔ cup

PEANUT BUTTER-BACON SPREAD

4 slices bacon
½ cup peanut butter
½ cup finely chopped dill pickle

2 tablespoons dill pickle juice
¼ teaspoon salt
Dash of hot pepper sauce

Cook bacon until crisp. Drain on paper towels. Crumble into small pieces. Mix with peanut butter, dill pickles, juice, and seasoning. Serve on crackers.

Yield: 1 cup

Soups

PEANUT BUTTER VEGETABLE POTAGE

1 10½-ounce can cream of
    mushroom soup
1 soup can water
¼ cup peanut butter
1 teaspoon celery salt

1 10½-ounce can
    vegetable soup
2 tablespoons fresh
    chopped chives

Combine mushroom soup, water, peanut butter, and celery salt in bowl, blending with beater. Stir in vegetable soup and chill. Serve sprinkled with chives.

Yield: 4 servings

QUICK PEANUT SOUP

¼ cup finely chopped
    onion
1 tablespoon butter
½ cup smooth peanut
    butter

1 10½-ounce can cream
    of chicken soup
1 10½-ounce can cream
    of celery soup
2 soup cans milk

Cook onion in butter in saucepan until tender but not browned. Stir in peanut butter and cook for several minutes more. Blend in soups and milk and heat.

Yield: 6 servings

CREAM OF PEANUT SOUP

1/4 cup butter
1 cup thinly sliced
    celery
1 medium onion,
    chopped fine
2 tablespoons flour

2 quarts chicken stock
    or broth
1 cup creamy peanut
    butter
1 cup light cream

Melt butter in large saucepan over low heat and add celery and onion. Cook until tender but not browned. Add flour and stir until mixture is smooth. Gradually add chicken broth and bring to a boil. Blend in peanut butter and simmer about 15 minutes. Stir in cream just before serving.

Yield: 8 servings

PEANUT CREOLE SOUP

1/2 cup chopped onion
2 tablespoons peanut oil
1 tablespoon flour
1 1/2 teaspoons salt

1/2 teaspoon celery salt
1/2 cup peanut butter
2 cups milk
2 cups tomato juice

Sauté onion in peanut oil until tender but not browned. Add flour and seasonings. Blend in peanut butter. Add milk gradually, stirring to blend. Cook and stir until mixture comes to a boil and is thickened. Add tomato juice and bring just to a boil. Serve hot.

Yield: 5 servings

Main Dishes

VEAL PERU

2 pounds boneless veal,
  cubed
Flour, salt and pepper
  for dusting
½ cup peanut oil
1 onion, chopped
1 clove garlic, chopped
3 cups stock or water
2 cups solid-pack
  tomatoes

½ cup peanut butter
1 teaspoon salt
⅛ teaspoon pepper
6 carrots, quartered
1 package frozen peas
2 tablespoons chopped
  parsley

Dust veal in flour seasoned with salt and pepper. Brown slowly in hot oil in large Dutch oven. Add onion and garlic and sauté 2–3 minutes. Pour off all fat, add stock, tomatoes, and peanut butter. Stir, and simmer covered for 1 hour, or until meat is tender. Add remaining ingredients and simmer 15–20 minutes more or until carrots are tender.

Yield: 6 servings

GROUNDNUT CHOP

¾ cup peanut butter
2 tablespoons corn oil
2 teaspoons salt
½ teaspoon paprika
¼ teaspoon nutmeg
¼ teaspoon pepper

2 cups water
3 cups cubed cooked
  chicken or lamb
  (about 1-inch cubes)
Rice ring

Selected accompaniments:
  flaked coconut, currants, chutney, slivered toasted almonds

Blend peanut butter and corn oil in skillet, then mix in salt, paprika, nutmeg, and pepper. Place over low heat and blend in water, stirring vigorously with wire whip or spoon. Add chicken or lamb. Cover and simmer, stirring occasionally, until thoroughly heated, about 10 minutes. Serve in ring of cooked rice with a variety of accompaniments.

Yield: 6 servings

BAKED HAM ROLLS

2 cups mashed sweet
   potatoes (1 1-pound
   can)
2 tablespoons margarine,
   melted
8 large thin slices
   cooked ham
1 cup dark corn syrup

½ cup creamy peanut
   butter
¼ cup orange juice
1 tablespoon margarine,
   melted
1 teaspoon grated orange
   rind

Combine mashed sweet potatoes and 2 tablespoons margarine. Place about ¼ cup mixture on each ham slice. Roll up and fasten with wooden picks. Place in shallow baking dish. Combine remaining ingredients. Pour over ham rolls. Bake in moderate oven (350°) until heated, about 30 minutes, basting and turning occasionally.

Yield: 4 servings

HAM SLICE WITH PEANUT BUTTER

1 slice ham, ½ inch
   thick
1 teaspoon prepared
   mustard

¼ cup peanut butter
4 tablespoons brown
   sugar
4 medium-ripe bananas

Put ham in flat casserole or baking dish. Spread with mustard and peanut butter and sprinkle with 2 tablespoons brown sugar. Bake in moderate oven (350°) 30 minutes. Arrange peeled bananas around ham, sprinkle with remaining 2 tablespoons brown sugar, and bake 10 minutes longer.

Yield: 4 servings

HAM GRILLED WITH PEANUT SAUCE

¼ cup peanut butter
¼ cup orange marmalade
2 tablespoons soy sauce

1 center-cut ham slice,
1½ pounds

Mix peanut butter, orange marmalade, and soy sauce. Spread both sides of ham slice with peanut butter mixture. Grill over charcoal about 10 minutes, turning to brown both sides.

Yield: 4 servings

SOUTHERN PORK CHOPS

4 pork loin chops
1 medium onion, cut in
    4 slices
¼ cup peanut butter
Half of a 10½-ounce
    can cream of
    mushroom soup

½ cup milk
1 teaspoon Worcestershire
    sauce
1 teaspoon salt
⅛ teaspoon pepper

Brown pork chops quickly on both sides in small amount of fat. Pour off excess fat and return pork chops to skillet.

Top each pork chop with an onion slice. Mix peanut butter with remaining ingredients. Pour over pork chops. Cover and cook over very low heat for about 45 minutes or until tender.

Yield: 4 servings

PORK CHOPS WITH MUSHROOMS

1 tablespoon corn oil	1 envelope onion
6 medium pork chops	soup mix
½ pound fresh	½ cup peanut butter
mushrooms, sliced	¼ cup chopped green
2½ cups water	pepper

Heat corn oil in large skillet. Add pork chops and cook over medium heat, turning once, until browned on both sides. Remove chops. Discard all but 1 tablespoon drippings. Brown mushrooms lightly in 1 tablespoon drippings in same skillet, using medium heat. Remove mushrooms. Stir water into drippings in skillet. Bring to boil. Stir in soup mix, peanut butter, and green pepper. Reduce heat, add chops. Cover and simmer until meat is tender, 45 to 50 minutes. Add mushrooms, heat thoroughly.

Yield: 4–6 servings

PORK ROAST
WITH BRAZILIAN PEANUT SAUCE

3 pounds loin or rib	1 quart stock or water
roast of pork	¾ cup peanut butter
1 onion, chopped	1 teaspoon salt
4 tomatoes, peeled and	⅛ teaspoon pepper
chopped	

Roast pork in slow oven (325°) about 1¼ hours or until well browned. Remove pork from pan, add onion, and sauté a few minutes. Pour off all fat and add remaining ingredients. Bring to a boil, stirring constantly. Add pork roast and simmer, covered, 20–30 minutes or until pork is done. Place meat on serving platter and keep hot. Beat sauce until smooth and serve over hot pork.

Yield: 4 servings

INDONESIAN PORK
AND PEANUT SAUCE

PORK:

1 pound pork
3 teaspoons boemboe sate*
1 tablespoon soy sauce

Cube pork and marinate for 1 hour with *boemboe sate* and soy sauce. Place on skewers. Broil. Serve with peanut sauce.

PEANUT SAUCE:

4 tablespoons peanut butter	1 tablespoon vinegar
¼ teaspoon sugar	2 teaspoons hot sauce
¼ teaspoon salt	1 cup milk

Stir ingredients well. Bring to boil and remove from heat at once. Serve hot with broiled pork.

Yield: 2–3 servings

* *Boemboe sate* is a thick, reddish-brown sauce that can be found in gourmet shops.

SPICY BEEF KABAB

2 pounds lean, boneless
beef
¼ cup smooth peanut
butter
1½ teaspoons ground
coriander
1½ teaspoons salt
½ teaspoon red pepper
1 teaspoon ground cumin

½ teaspoon freshly
ground black pepper
4 medium-sized onions,
grated
1 clove garlic, minced
1½ tablespoons lemon
juice
1 tablespoon brown sugar
3 tablespoons soy sauce

Cut beef into 1½-inch cubes. Mix peanut butter with remaining ingredients in a medium-sized bowl. Add beef cubes. Stir until cubes are coated on all sides. Cover and let stand in refrigerator for several hours.

When ready to cook put cubes on skewers. Broil in broiler or over charcoal 15–20 minutes, turning to brown on both sides. Serve with chilled mandarin orange sections if desired.

Yield: 6 servings
Pork may be substituted for beef in this recipe.

HOLIDAY BURGERS

1 egg
¼ cup chili sauce
1 teaspoon salt
¼ teaspoon pepper
1–1½ teaspoons chili
powder
¼ cup grated onion
1 pound ground beef

6 tablespoons peanut
butter
6 slices process
American cheese
6 buns
Pimiento
Stuffed green olives

Combine egg, chili sauce, salt, pepper, chili powder, and onion in bowl. Add beef and mix lightly until blended. Form into 6 flat patties. Top each patty with 1 tablespoon peanut butter. Cut cheese slices in half and arrange crisscross on top of patties. Pan-fry in a small amount of fat 3–4 minutes. Cover and cook 2–3 minutes longer to melt cheese. Serve on buns, garnish each burger with piece of pimiento and of olive.

Yield: 6 patties

PEANUT BUTTER MEAT BALLS

½ cup peanut butter
½ pound ground beef
¼ cup finely chopped onion
2 tablespoons chili sauce
1 teaspoon salt

⅛ teaspoon pepper
1 egg, beaten
2 tablespoons peanut oil
2 cups seasoned tomato sauce

Mix peanut butter lightly with beef, onion, chili sauce, salt, pepper, and egg.

Form into 12 meat balls. Brown in hot peanut oil. Add tomato sauce, cover, and simmer about 30 minutes. Serve with cooked rice or spaghetti.

Yield: 4 servings

BEEF BIRMINGHAM

2 tablespoons peanut oil
1 clove garlic, sliced
1 pound beef chuck, cut in thin strips
1 cup sliced onions (3 medium)
1 cup sliced celery
2 tablespoons peanut butter

2 tablespoons soy sauce
½ teaspoon sugar
1 cup beef stock or bouillon cube and water
Dash of fresh ground pepper

Heat oil in skillet. Add garlic, beef, onions, and celery. Sauté quickly until lightly browned. Reduce heat and add remaining ingredients. Cover and simmer over low heat 1 hour or until meat is tender. Add more liquid during cooking if needed.

Serve over hot cooked rice or noodles.

Yield: 4 servings

PEANUT BUTTER-BEEF MEAT LOAF

½ cup peanut butter
½ cup dry bread crumbs
½ cup tomato sauce
1 teaspoon salt
⅛ teaspoon pepper

1 egg, slightly beaten
¼ cup finely chopped onion
¾ pound ground beef

Combine peanut butter, crumbs, tomato sauce, seasonings, egg, and onion and mix until blended. Add meat and mix lightly. Shape into loaf and place on greased flat pan. Bake in moderate oven (350°) 1 hour. Serve with gravy made from drippings or chili sauce.

Yield: 4 servings

MEAT ROLL MONTGOMERY

1 egg, slightly beaten	*1 pound ground beef*
½ cup milk	*½ pound ground pork*
½ cup bread crumbs	*2 cups mashed potatoes*
1½ teaspoons salt	*¼ cup peanut butter*
¼ teaspoon pepper	*1 medium onion, grated*
1 teaspoon Worcestershire	
sauce	

Combine egg, milk, bread crumbs, salt, pepper, and Worcestershire sauce. Let soak for 10 minutes. Add meats and mix lightly. On a sheet of waxed paper, shape meat mixture into a rectangle about ¾ inch thick.

Combine potatoes, peanut butter, and grated onion. Season to taste with salt and pepper. Spread on top of meat. Roll up in jelly-roll fashion and place in a greased shallow baking pan. Bake in a moderate oven (375°) 1 hour.

Yield: 8 servings

BRAZILIAN BEEFSTEAK

2 pounds beef round steak,	*¾ cup chopped onion*
sliced ¾ inch thick	*1½ cups solid-pack*
¼ cup flour	*tomatoes*
1 teaspoon salt	*1 cup chicken or beef*
⅛ teaspoon fresh	*stock*
ground pepper	*½ cup peanut butter*
4 tablespoons cooking oil	

Cut steak into 6 servings. Mix flour with salt and pepper and coat meat with flour.

Heat oil in large skillet and brown meat on both sides. Remove meat and sauté onion until tender but not browned.

Return meat to skillet. Add tomatoes and stock. Cover and cook over low heat 15 minutes. Stir in peanut butter and continue cooking 15 minutes or until meat is tender. Serve with rice.

Yield: 6 servings

GROUNDNUT STEW

2 pounds lamb stewing
  meat
3 large onions, sliced
1½ teaspoons salt
3 cups water
3 large tomatoes,
  quartered

3 chili peppers, washed
  and seeded*
1 cup peanut butter
2 cups bouillon
3–4 cups hot cooked
  rice
6 hard-cooked eggs

Combine stew meat and onions in a large saucepan. Add salt and water and cook over low heat for about 1 hour or until meat begins to get tender.

In another pan, combine tomatoes and chili peppers with ½ cup additional water. Cover and cook for 8–10 minutes, or until tomatoes and peppers are tender. Strain. Mix peanut butter, tomatoes, and bouillon and add to meat. Continue cooking over low heat until meat is tender.

When ready to serve, put rice in plate, a hard-cooked egg in the center of the rice, and spoon stew and gravy over.

Yield: 6 servings

* If fresh chili peppers are not available, use dried peppers or those pickled in vinegar.

CHICKEN PUNJAB

⅓ cup cornstarch
2 teaspoons paprika
½ teaspoon salt
½ teaspoon onion salt
1 broiler-fryer chicken,
2½ pounds, cut in
serving pieces
¾ cup peanut oil
1 medium onion, minced
1 cup sliced celery
1 green pepper, cut in
rings

1½ cups uncooked
converted rice
½ cup chunky peanut
butter
2 tablespoons soy sauce
2 tablespoons brown
sugar
¾ cup water
¼ cup seedless raisins
1 can (1 pound 4
ounces) pineapple
chunks with syrup

Combine cornstarch, paprika, salt, and onion salt in clean paper bag. Add chicken pieces two or three at a time and shake until well coated. Heat ½ cup of the oil in large Dutch oven or extra-large skillet with cover. Add chicken pieces and cook over moderate heat until well browned, turning as needed, about 15 minutes. Remove chicken. Add remaining oil and heat, add onion, celery, and green pepper and toss over moderate heat until softened. Add rice and toss to blend and coat with mixture. Into peanut butter gradually stir the soy sauce, brown sugar, and water. Add with raisins and pineapple chunks and syrup to rice mixture. Stir to combine and bring to boil. Reduce heat to simmer. Place browned chicken on top. Cover and cook slowly 40 minutes or until rice tastes done. Every 10 minutes raise cover and lift rice from bottom to prevent sticking and add a little more water if needed. Before serving, taste rice and add more salt and soy sauce if desired. Prettiest if rice is heaped on platter and chicken arranged around' and upon it.

Yield: 5 generous servings

CHICKEN WITH PEANUT SAUCE

1 broiler-fryer chicken,
  2½ to 3 pounds, cut
  in serving pieces
¼ cup seasoned flour
½ cup vegetable oil
2 tablespoons minced
  onion
3 cups chicken stock or
  water

½ cup sherry if desired
1 small piece cinnamon
  stick
1 teaspoon sugar
½ teaspoon salt
Dash of garlic powder
½ cup peanut butter
2 tablespoons cornstarch

Dust chicken in flour seasoned with salt and pepper. Fry chicken slowly in hot oil in a 10-inch aluminum skillet 20–25 minutes or until pieces are well browned. Add onion and sauté 2–3 minutes. Pour off all oil from the frying pan. Add chicken stock and sherry if desired, cinnamon, sugar, salt, garlic powder and keep hot. Add peanut butter to gravy, blending in well. Stir cornstarch to a smooth paste with 2 tablespoons water; gradually stir into gravy. Cook, stirring constantly, until gravy thickens and boils 1 minute. Serve hot over chicken with hot fluffy rice.

Yield: 4 servings

INDONESIAN CHICKEN

½ cup diced or ground
  onions
2 cloves garlic, minced
½ teaspoon dried
  ground chili pepper
½ cup peanut butter
1 teaspoon salt
2 teaspoons oil

2 tablespoons soy sauce
1 cup water
2 tablespoons lemon or
  lime juice
2 broiler-fryer chickens,
  2½ to 3 pounds, cut
  in quarters

Combine onion, garlic, chili pepper, peanut butter, and salt. Sauté in oil 3 minutes. Add soy sauce, water, and lemon juice and cook at low heat 5 minutes. Cool. Marinate chicken in sauce 1 hour, then broil 25–30 minutes, turning the chicken several times and brushing with marinade each time. Heat remaining marinade and serve as a sauce over cooked chicken.

Yield: 8 servings

BAKED PEANUT BUTTER CHICKEN

1 broiler-fryer chicken, 2½ to 3 pounds, cut in serving pieces	1 teaspoon salt
	⅛ teaspoon pepper
	⅓ cup milk
¼ cup flour	½ cup dry bread crumbs
1 egg	¼ cup peanut oil
⅓ cup peanut butter	

Wash and dry chicken pieces. Dip in flour. Blend egg with peanut butter, salt, and pepper. Gradually add milk, beating with fork to blend. Dip floured chicken in peanut butter mixture and then in crumbs. Place on oiled flat baking pan. Drizzle remaining oil over chicken pieces. Bake in a moderate oven (375°) 45 minutes or until tender.

Yield: 4 servings

CHICKEN WITH PEANUT BUTTER BARBECUE SAUCE

½ cup peanut butter
¼ cup honey
¼ cup soy sauce
1 onion, grated
1 clove garlic, chopped
    fine

1 cup beef broth
¼ teaspoon fresh
    ground black pepper
2 broiler-fryer chickens,
    2½ to 3 pounds,
    quartered

Combine peanut butter, honey, soy sauce, onion, garlic, broth, and pepper, stirring to blend. Place quartered chickens in flat pan and spread with half the sauce. Let stand for several hours in refrigerator. Cook over coals or under broiler, basting with remainder of sauce, until tender, about 30–40 minutes.

Yield: 8 servings

CHICKEN SAUTÉ WITH PEANUT ORANGE SAUCE

1 broiler-fryer chicken,
    2½ to 3 pounds, cut
    in serving pieces
1 teaspoon salt
¼ teaspoon freshly
    ground pepper

½ teaspoon onion salt
1 teaspoon paprika
2 tablespoons peanut oil
¼ cup peanut butter
1 cup orange juice

Wash and dry chicken pieces. Mix salt, pepper, onion salt, and paprika and rub into chicken pieces. Heat oil in an aluminum skillet over medium heat. Sauté the chicken pieces until nicely browned on all sides. Cover. Reduce heat and continue cooking about 25 minutes or until chicken is tender. Remove chicken to platter. Drain excess fat from skillet, add peanut butter, and cook and stir for several minutes. Add orange juice to skillet and bring to a boil. Spoon peanut orange sauce over chicken.

Yield: 3–4 servings

FAR EAST CHICKEN BARBECUE

½ cup diced or ground
 onion
2 cloves garlic, minced
½ teaspoon dried
 ground chili pepper
½ cup peanut butter
1 teaspoon salt
2 teaspoons peanut oil

2 tablespoons soy sauce
1 cup water
2 tablespoons lemon or
 lime juice
2 broiler-fryer chickens,
 2½ pounds, cut in
 quarters

Combine onion, garlic, chili pepper, peanut butter, and salt. Sauté in peanut oil 3 minutes. Add soy sauce, water, and lemon juice and cook at low heat 5 minutes. Cool. Marinate chicken in sauce for an hour, then broil 25–30 minutes, turning the chicken several times and brushing with marinade each time. Heat remaining marinade and serve as a sauce over cooked chicken.

Yield: 8 servings

PEANUT CHICKEN SALAD

1 7-ounce can chicken,
minced
¼ cup crunchy peanut
butter

2 tablespoons mayonnaise
¼ cup chopped stuffed
olives

Combine all ingredients. Pack into 6-ounce container with cover. Place in refrigerator until ready to serve on lettuce cups. *Yield: 2 servings.*

CHICKEN AND SEAFOOD INDONESIA

1 4-pound chicken,
cleaned
8 cups water
2 leeks

1 bay leaf
2 sprigs parsley
2 teaspoons salt

Step 1: Put chicken in a pot, cover with water. Add remaining ingredients and cook 1½ hours or until tender. Strain stock and reduce to 4 cups. Remove meat from bone. Cut into strips. This may be done on day prior to serving dish.

½ cup peanut oil
1¼ cups chopped onion
2 cloves garlic, minced
2 cups chopped cooked
shrimp
1 cup cooked crab meat
1 cup cooked ham
1 teaspoon salt
2 teaspoons ground
coriander

1 teaspoon ground cumin
½ teaspoon ground
red pepper
¼ teaspoon nutmeg
4 tablespoons peanut
butter
4 cups chicken stock
1½ cups rice

Step 2: Heat peanut oil in large casserole. Add onion and garlic and sauté until tender but not browned. Add chicken, shrimp, crab meat, ham, seasonings and peanut butter. Cook 10 minutes. Add 4 cups chicken stock and rice. Cover. Continue cooking 12–15 minutes or until rice is tender and fluffy. Season to taste with additional salt and pepper.

Yield: 6–8 servings

SHRIMP TAHITI

2 tablespoons peanut oil	1 8-ounce can tomato sauce
1¼ cups diced onion	
2 tomatoes, peeled and diced	2 pounds raw shrimp, peeled
2 teaspoons salt	½ cup hot water
¼ teaspoon crushed red pepper	½ cup chunk-style peanut butter
½ bay leaf	3 cups hot cooked rice

Heat peanut oil in large skillet, add onion, and sauté over low heat until tender but not browned. Add tomatoes, salt, red pepper, bay leaf, and tomato sauce. Cover and simmer 15 minutes. Add shrimp. Blend hot water with peanut butter and add to mixture. Cover and simmer 10 minutes longer. Serve over rice.

Yield: 6 servings

DIXIE FRENCH TOAST

½ cup peanut butter
8 slices crisp bacon,
  crumbled
12 slices white bread

2 bananas
2 eggs
1 cup milk
¼ teaspoon salt

Combine peanut butter and bacon and spread each slice of bread with about 1 tablespoon of the mixture. Slice bananas and place on half of the prepared bread, using ⅓ banana per sandwich. Close sandwiches. Beat eggs, milk, and salt together. Dip closed sandwiches in the mixture and brown in a little hot cooking oil. Serve with strawberry jam.

Yield: 6 servings

CREOLE CHEESE LOAF

1¼ cups crunchy
  peanut butter
1¼ cups cooked baby
  lima beans
2 tablespoons finely
  chopped onion
1 teaspoon salt
¼ teaspoon pepper
1¼ cups soft bread
  crumbs

1½ cups grated
  American cheese
1¼ cups milk
1 tablespoon chopped
  parsley
3 eggs, well beaten
1½ cups well-seasoned
  tomato sauce

Combine all ingredients except tomato sauce, mixing well. Spoon into a greased loaf pan 9×5×2½ inches. Bake in a moderate oven (350°) 35–40 minutes. Serve hot with tomato sauce.   *Yield:* 8 servings

PEANUT BUTTER POTATO SALAD

¼ cup vinegar
¼ cup peanut oil
1 teaspoon salt
¼ teaspoon pepper
3 cups diced hot,
    cooked potatoes
1 cup diced celery

¼ cup chopped green
    onions
1 cup diced ham
½ cup mayonnaise
½ cup smooth or
    crunchy peanut butter

Combine vinegar, oil, salt, and pepper in bowl. Add hot
diced potatoes and mix lightly. Chill.

When ready to serve add celery, onions, and ham. Combine
mayonnaise and peanut butter. Add to potato mixture and
toss lightly.

Yield: about 6 cups

WAFFLES

½ cup peanut butter
¼ cup shortening
2 eggs, beaten
1½ cups milk
1¾ cups sifted
    all-purpose flour

3 teaspoons baking
    powder
¼ teaspoon salt
3 tablespoons sugar

Cream together peanut butter and shortening. Blend in
eggs and milk. Sift dry ingredients together and add to peanut butter mixture, beating until smooth. Pour batter into
preheated waffle baker and bake until waffle stops steaming
or until signal light on baker indicates waffle is done.

Yield: 4–6 servings

PEANUT BUTTER PIZZA

1 cup warm water
1 package or cake yeast, active dry or compressed
1 teaspoon sugar
1 teaspoon salt
4 tablespoons peanut oil
3¼ cups unsifted flour (about)
1 cup chopped green pepper
⅔ cup chopped onion
2 cloves garlic, finely chopped
2 cups tomato sauce
½ teaspoon orégano
½ teaspoon basil
½ teaspoon chili powder
½ teaspoon salt
¼ teaspoon pepper
3 cups grated Cheddar cheese
½ cup peanut butter

Measure warm water into large warm bowl. Sprinkle or crumble in yeast. Stir until dissolved. Add sugar, 1 teaspoon salt, 2 tablespoons peanut oil, and half the flour. Beat until smooth. Stir in enough additional flour to form a soft dough. Turn out onto lightly floured board and knead until smooth and elastic, about 8–10 minutes. Place in greased bowl, turning to grease top. Cover. Let rise in warm place, free from draft, until doubled in bulk, about 45 minutes.

Meanwhile prepare filling. Place green pepper, onion, garlic, and remaining 2 tablespoons peanut oil in top of double boiler and cook until tender. Add tomato sauce, orégano, basil, chili powder, ½ teaspoon salt, and pepper. Cover. Cook over low heat 10 minutes, stirring occasionally. Add grated cheese and peanut butter. Cook over boiling water until cheese is melted and mixture blended. Punch dough down. Divide in half. On a lightly floured board, roll each half into a circle to fit a 12-inch pizza pan. Place each in a greased pan and press around rim of pan to form a standing rim of dough. Spread filling on dough. Bake in hot oven (400°) 25 minutes or until done. Cut and serve.

Yield: 2 pizzas

PEANUT BUTTER TURKEY STUFFING

3½ quarts day-old
   bread cubes (about
   1½ loaves)
⅔ cup finely chopped
   onion
1 tablespoon salt

¼ teaspoon pepper
Giblets, chopped
2½ cups milk
1 cup crunchy peanut
   butter
½ cup raisins

Combine bread cubes, onion, salt, pepper, and giblets in a large bowl. In a saucepan, heat the milk, peanut butter, and raisins, stirring constantly until the peanut butter is soft.

Pour peanut butter mixture over the bread and toss lightly with a fork. Stuff turkey or other fowl lightly, taking care not to pack stuffing too tightly.

Yield: stuffing for 12–16 pound turkey

THE JOHN ZINK SPECIAL
(BROILED STEAK WITH PEANUT BUTTER)

¼ cup melted butter
Juice 1 lemon
2 1-pound club steaks 2
   inches thick

Seasoned salt
Dash of pepper
Smooth peanut butter

Combine melted butter with lemon juice and brush generously on one side of steak. Cover with seasoned salt and pepper.

Broil about 5 inches from hottest flame or fire for 15 minutes. Turn, brush with butter-juice mixture, cover with seasoned salt, and broil for 10 minutes.

Slather with smooth peanut butter and return to broiler for about 5 minutes, or until peanut butter bubbles and is tinged with dark brown edges.

Cut steaks in 2 servings each and serve immediately.

Yield: 4 servings

Vegetables

CARROTS AND CELERY
SOUTHERN STYLE

2 tablespoons peanut oil
2 tablespoons flour
1 tablespoon peanut
  butter
¼ teaspoon salt
Dash of pepper

1 cup milk
½ cup chopped peanuts
1½ cups cooked sliced
  carrots, drained
1½ cups cooked sliced
  celery, drained

Blend oil, flour, peanut butter, salt, and pepper. Gradually stir in milk. Stir over low heat until thick and smooth. Mix with peanuts and vegetables. Pour into serving dish and sprinkle with more peanuts if desired.

Yield: 4 servings

FRIED CAULIFLOWER
WITH PEANUT BUTTER SAUCE

1 medium head
  cauliflower, separated
  into flowerets
¼ cup margarine
½ cup peanut butter
¼ cup mayonnaise

1 tablespoon sugar
1 tablespoon lemon juice
1 teaspoon chili sauce
⅛ teaspoon hot pepper
  sauce

Parboil cauliflower. Drain. Melt margarine in skillet. Add cauliflower and sauté until lightly browned. Drain. Combine peanut butter, mayonnaise, sugar, lemon juice, chili sauce, and hot pepper sauce in bowl. Spoon on top of hot cauliflower and serve immediately.

Yield: 4 servings

BRAISED CELERY WITH PEANUT-SOY SAUCE

3 cups sliced celery
1 medium onion, sliced
¼ cup water

¼ cup peanut butter
2 tablespoons soy sauce

Combine celery, onion, and water in 1-quart saucepan. Cover and cook 5–8 minutes. Remove celery and onion to warmed vegetable dish and keep hot. Add peanut butter and soy sauce to liquid left in pan. Cook and stir to blend and heat. Add 3–4 tablespoons of water to thin sauce. Pour sauce over cooked celery and onion.

Yield: 4–6 servings

SWEET POTATO PEANUT CASSEROLE

2 cups mashed sweet
  potatoes (1-pound
  can)
½ cup crushed pineapple,
  well drained
⅓ cup chunky peanut
  butter

2 tablespoons margarine,
  melted
¼ cup sugar
½ teaspoon salt
½ pound sliced bacon,
  partially cooked

Combine sweet potatoes, pineapple, peanut butter, margarine, sugar, and salt. Spoon into greased shallow casserole. Arrange bacon slices on top. Bake in moderate oven (350°) until mixture is hot and bacon is cooked, 30–45 minutes.

Yield: 4 servings

STUFFED SWEET POTATOES
WITH PEANUT BUTTER

4 medium-sized baked
    sweet potatoes
⅔ cup milk
¼ cup peanut butter

¼ teaspoon salt
Pepper
⅓ cup chopped salted
    peanuts

Cut hot baked sweet potatoes in half and remove from shells. Mash thoroughly. Add milk, peanut butter, and seasonings. Beat until fluffy and refill shells. Brown on a baking sheet at 425°. Sprinkle chopped peanuts on the top before browning.

Yield: 4 servings

SWEET POTATO BALLS

2 cups warm mashed
    potatoes
1 egg, beaten
2 tablespoons sugar

½ teaspoon salt
½ cup peanut butter
½ cup crushed cereal
    flakes or bread crumbs

Combine warm potatoes with beaten egg, sugar, and salt. Form into balls with peanut butter inside each one. Roll in crushed cereal flakes or bread crumbs. Place on greased baking sheet, bake in moderate oven (375°) about 20 minutes.

Yield: 4 servings

PEANUT BUTTER
JELLY SURPRISE SWEET POTATOES

Select medium-sized sweet potatoes to bake. Scrub and bake in a moderate oven (375°) 45 minutes. Cut a slice off top and scoop out centers. Mash with milk and season with salt and pepper. Fill shell half full. Put in a tablespoon each of peanut butter and jelly. Fill with remaining sweet potato mixture. Return to oven for 10–15 minutes.

BAKED STUFFED TOMATOES DOTHAN

6 ripe medium-sized
   tomatoes
½ cup smooth or
   crunchy peanut butter
¾ cup soft bread crumbs
1 teaspoon salt
⅛ teaspoon freshly
   ground pepper
½ teaspoon orégano
2 tablespoons finely
   chopped onion
¼ cup finely diced celery

Remove stem end from tomatoes. Cut a thin slice from top. With a spoon remove tomato pulp and chop. Mix with peanut butter and remaining ingredients. Fill tomato shells.

Place in a greased flat baking dish and bake in a hot oven (400°) 25–30 minutes. *Yield:* 6 servings

INDONESIAN VEGETABLE PLATTER

SALAD:

½ cup shredded raw
   cabbage
½ cup sliced raw carrots
½ cup cooked green beans
1 tomato, sliced
Lettuce leaves
1 cucumber, sliced
2 hard-cooked eggs, sliced

Arrange vegetables on a platter. (Indonesian cooks make each separate vegetable look like a flower.) Garnish with sliced eggs.

DRESSING:

6 tablespoons peanut butter	1 slice lemon
1 clove garlic, crushed	Salt to taste
1 teaspoon ground or crushed red pepper	1 cup water
1 teaspoon sugar	
1 laurel or bay leaf	½ cup milk

Sauté the peanut butter, garlic, and seasonings. Add water, sugar, and milk gradually. Cook on low flame, stirring continuously, until thickened. Serve the warm dressing separately.

Yield: 2 servings

Sauces and Dressings

SAUCE FOR MEAT

1 tablespoon margarine
½ cup finely chopped
  green pepper
⅓ cup finely chopped
  onion
1 medium tomato, pared
  and thinly sliced
2 tablespoons peanut
  butter

1 cup milk
Hamburgers or steaks
1 hard-cooked egg,
  chopped
1 tablespoon finely
  chopped parsley

Melt margarine in saucepan. Add green pepper, onion, and tomato. Cook over low heat 10 minutes, stirring frequently and breaking up tomato slices. Blend in peanut butter. Gradually add milk, stirring constantly. Cook until sauce is thickened slightly. Serve over hamburgers or steak. Sprinkle with chopped egg and parsley.

Yield: 1½ cups

BARBECUE SAUCE SAVANNAH

¼ cup smooth peanut
  butter
1 clove garlic, grated
1 medium onion, grated
1 tablespoon cider
  vinegar
1 tablespoon sugar

1 tablespoon soy sauce
¼ teaspoon crushed red
  pepper
1 8-ounce can tomato
  sauce
1 cup water
1 bouillon cube

Mix peanut butter with garlic, onion, vinegar, sugar, and seasonings. Gradually stir in tomato sauce and water, stirring to blend. Add bouillon cube. Bring to a boil and simmer over low heat 5 minutes.

Use as a marinade and basting sauce for pork or chicken.

Yield: 2½ cups

SPAGHETTI SAUCE

2 tablespoons corn oil
¼ cup finely chopped
  onion
¼ cup finely chopped
  green pepper
2½ cups water

1 4-ounce can tomato
  paste
½ teaspoon salt
¼ teaspoon orégano
2 bay leaves
½ cup peanut butter

Heat corn oil in skillet. Add onion and green pepper. Sauté until tender. Add water, tomato paste, salt, orégano, and bay leaves. Bring to boil. Mix in peanut butter. Cover and simmer about 30 minutes to blend.

Yield: 3 cups

VEGETABLE SAUCE

1 tablespoon margarine
¼ cup peanut butter
1 tablespoon flour

½ teaspoon salt
Dash of pepper
1¼ cups milk

Melt margarine in small saucepan over medium heat. Blend in peanut butter, then stir in flour, salt, and pepper. Gradually stir in milk. Cook, stirring constantly, until mixture thickens and comes to boil. Simmer 1 minute. Serve over cauliflower, green beans, onions, or lima beans.

Yield: 1 cup

PEANUT BUTTER CHANTILLY

¼ cup smooth or crunchy   *1 teaspoon salt*
   peanut butter   *Dash of pepper*
½ pint dairy sour cream   *1 tablespoon lemon juice*
1 tablespoon horse-radish

Put peanut butter in small bowl. Gradually mix in sour cream until blended. Fold in remaining ingredients. Serve with cooked broccoli, green beans, asparagus, carrots, or other cooked vegetables.

Yield: 1¼ cups

HEARTY SAUCE PIQUANTE

⅓ cup peanut butter
⅔ cup milk

Combine peanut butter and milk, stirring to blend. Heat and serve over cooked broccoli, carrots, asparagus, cauliflower.

Yield: 1 cup

VARIATIONS:

1. Add 2 tablespoons chopped parsley or chives
2. Add ½ teaspoon chili powder
3. Add 1 tablespoon tomato purée

STRAWBERRY PEANUT DRESSING.

½ cup peanut butter
¼ cup mayonnaise
½ cup strawberry jam

3 tablespoons lemon juice
Dash of salt

Combine all ingredients, mixing lightly to blend. Chill. Serve as dressing with fruit salad.

Yield: 1½ cups dressing

PEANUT SALAD DRESSING

2 tablespoons smooth
   peanut butter
¼ cup cider vinegar
2 tablespoons water

1 envelope old-fashioned
   French salad dressing
   mix
⅔ cup salad oil

Combine peanut butter, cider vinegar, water, and dressing. Mix in a container. Cover and shake until blended. Add oil and shake again.

Serve with vegetable or fruit salads.

Yield: 1 cup

PEANUT BUTTER CHEESE DRESSING

½ cup peanut butter
1 3½-ounce package
   cream cheese
2 tablespoons honey or
   sugar

1 tablespoon lemon juice
Dash of salt
¾ cup pineapple juice

Combine peanut butter with cream cheese. Add honey, lemon juice, and salt. Gradually stir in pineapple juice, blending well. Chill. Serve as dressing with fruit salad.

Yield: 1½ cups

FLUFFY PEANUT BUTTER FRUIT DRESSING

½ cup peanut butter   1 tablespoon lemon juice
½ cup marshmallow fluff   Dash of salt
½ cup orange or
    pineapple juice

Blend peanut butter with marshmallow fluff. Gradually fold in orange and lemon juice, stirring to blend. Stir in salt. Store in covered container in refrigerator. Serve with fruit salads.

Yield: 1⅓ cups

Sandwiches

SAVANNAH SANDWICH LOAF

1 loaf French or Italian
   bread
1½ cups bread crumbs
½ cup water
1 tablespoon chopped
   parsley
½ cup finely chopped
   onion
¾ teaspoon salt

¼ teaspoon pepper
½ teaspoon Worcestershire
   sauce
¼ cup crunchy peanut
   butter
2 egg yolks or 1 whole
   egg
¾ pound ground beef

Cut a V-shaped piece lengthwise from the top of loaf of French or Italian bread. Remove piece and with a fork pull out soft bread crumbs from inside of loaf so that an inch shell of bread and crust remains.

Measure 1½ cups crumbs and mix with water, parsley, onion, seasonings, peanut butter, egg yolks, and meat. Pile lightly into bread shell, cover with top crust, and tie tightly with string in about 3 places. Wrap in aluminum foil and bake in a moderate oven (350°) 1 hour. Cut into inch-thick slices and serve hot. It may be cooled in foil and chilled in refrigerator and served cold.

Yield: 8–10 sandwiches

NASI GORENG SANDWICH

¾ cup peanut butter
¼ teaspoon crushed red
  pepper
¾ teaspoon ginger
½ cup raisins
½ cup mayonnaise
¼ teaspoon coriander
¼ teaspoon cumin
⅛ teaspoon turmeric
¼ teaspoon salt
Dash of pepper

1 cup diced cooked
  shrimp
1 cup finely diced celery
15 slices white toast
1 medium onion, sliced in
  rings
1 large green pepper,
  sliced in rings
Butter
3 hard-cooked eggs, sliced
5 lettuce leaves

Combine peanut butter, crushed red pepper, ginger, and raisins. Combine mayonnaise, coriander, cumin, turmeric, salt and pepper, mixing well. Add shrimp and celery and mix. Spread peanut butter mixture on 5 slices of toast. Arrange onion rings and green pepper rings on top of peanut butter. Place a slice of buttered toast on top. Spread ¼ cup of shrimp mixture on toast. Arrange sliced hard-cooked eggs on top of shrimp and top with lettuce and slice of buttered toast. Cut sandwiches into quarters. Serve immediately.

Yield: 5 sandwiches

RING-AROUNDS

½ cup peanut butter
⅓ cup chili sauce
2 tablespoons prepared
  mustard

½ cup chopped lettuce
4 pickle slices
4 slices round bread

Mix peanut butter with chili sauce and mustard. Spread bread with peanut butter mixture. Ring with chopped lettuce and center with a pickle slice.

Yield: 4 servings

BROILED TEEN SPECIAL

½ cup peanut butter	8 slices bread
2 tablespoons mayonnaise	Mayonnaise or soft butter
5 slices bacon, cooked and crumbled	3 large tomatoes, sliced
	8 slices American cheese

Combine peanut butter, mayonnaise, and bacon. Toast bread lightly. Spread each slice of toasted bread with mayonnaise or butter. Place 2 slices of tomato on each slice of bread, and then a slice of cheese. Spread a rounding tablespoon of peanut butter mixture over the cheese. Broil until lightly browned, about 2 minutes.

Yield: 8 open-faced sandwiches

EASY PIZZAS

¼ cup peanut butter	4 English muffins, split in half and lightly toasted
⅓ cup chili sauce	
1 tablespoon prepared mustard	Mozzarella cheese
8 slices salami or pressed ham	Grated Parmesan cheese if desired

Combine peanut butter, chili sauce, and mustard. Place a slice of meat on muffin half. Spread a rounding tablespoon of peanut butter mixture over meat. Scatter pieces of *mozzarella* cheese over the top and sprinkle with Parmesan cheese. Bake in hot oven (450°) 8–10 minutes until cheese browns lightly.

Yield: 8 pizzas

PEANUT BUTTER GRILLWICHES

8 slices bread
½ cup peanut butter
8 slices cooked bacon, cut
   in half crosswise
¼ cup strawberry jelly
Softened butter

Spread 4 slices of bread with peanut butter and top with 4 pieces (2 slices) of bacon. Spread remaining bread with jelly and put on peanut butter slices, jelly side down. Spread outside with softened butter.

Heat an aluminum electric skillet to medium heat. Put sandwiches in skillet and cook golden brown (about 2 minutes). Turn and brown on other side.

Yield: 4 sandwiches

EASY-AS-PIE PEANUT BUTTER
APPLE SANDWICHES

½ cup peanut butter
¼ teaspoon apple-pie
   spice
2 teaspoons brown sugar
1 red eating apple
Juice of ½ lemon
4 slices bread
4 slices sharp American
   process cheese

Mix peanut butter, apple-pie spice, and sugar. Wash apple, remove core, and cut into 8–12 very thin slices, including peel. Dip in lemon juice. Toast bread lightly. Spread with butter, then with peanut butter mixture. Top with apple slices, then with cheese. Toast 5 inches from heat source in preheated broiler 1 minute or until cheese melts and cloaks apple slices.

Yield: 4 servings

PEANUT BUTTER PINEAPPLE SANDWICH

1 cup crunchy peanut butter
¾ cup drained crushed pineapple
½ cup honey

½ cup finely diced celery
⅛ teaspoon salt
1–2 tablespoons pineapple juice if necessary

Mix all ingredients together until well blended. Add pineapple juice if necessary to make mixture soft enough to spread. Makes 2¼ cups, or enough for 9–10 sandwiches. Spread may be refrigerated and kept for several weeks.

Yield: 9–10 sandwiches

YUMMY MALLOW SANDWICHES

¾ cup peanut butter
12 slices bread
2 large bananas, sliced

Butter
¾ cup marshmallow fluff

Spread peanut butter on half the bread. Arrange bananas on peanut butter. Spread remaining bread with butter and then with marshmallow fluff. Put sandwiches together and cut into quarters.

Yield: 6 sandwiches

PEANUT CHEESE SANDWICH SPREAD

½ cup peanut butter
½ cup creamed cottage
cheese
3 tablespoons French
dressing

¼ cup chopped stuffed
olives
1 teaspoon onion salt

Mix all ingredients together lightly. Use as a spread for sandwiches or crackers.

Yield: 1¼ cups

DEVILED PEANUT BUTTER FILLING

½ cup peanut butter
1 medium tomato,
peeled and chopped
1 hard-cooked egg,
chopped
¼ cup finely chopped
celery
1 tablespoon mayonnaise

1 tablespoon vinegar
1 teaspoon prepared
mustard
½ teaspoon
Worcestershire sauce
½ teaspoon salt
Dash of pepper

Combine all ingredients and mix lightly to blend. Use as a spread for open-faced or closed sandwiches.

Yield: 1½ cups

Breads

PEANUT BUTTER BREAD

4½ cups sifted flour
6 teaspoons baking powder
1¼ teaspoons salt
⅔ cup sugar
1 cup peanut butter

2 eggs, well beaten
2 cups milk
1 tablespoon grated orange rind
½ cup chopped salted peanuts

Sift flour with baking powder, salt, and sugar. Cut in peanut butter with 2 knives or pastry blender until mixture is like corn meal.

Combine eggs, milk, and orange rind and stir with chopped peanuts into flour mixture until blended. Grease bottom and sides of a loaf pan 10×5×4 inches. Pour batter into pan. Bake in moderate oven (350°) 1 hour or until done. Remove from pan. Cool. When cold, wrap in foil and store overnight before cutting.

Yield: 1 loaf

PEANUT BUTTER GARLIC BREAD

¼ cup smooth or crunchy peanut butter
¼ cup softened margarine

1 clove garlic, crushed
⅛ teaspoon salt
1 loaf French bread

Mix peanut butter with margarine, garlic, and salt. Slice French bread in 1-inch slices not quite through bottom of loaf. Spread peanut butter mixture between slices. Wrap in aluminum foil and bake in hot oven (400°) 10–15 minutes. Serve hot.

Yield: 6–8 servings

PEANUT BUTTER APPLE MUFFINS

2 cups sifted flour	¼ cup shortening
4 teaspoons baking powder	¼ cup peanut butter
¾ teaspoon salt	¼ cup sugar
½ teaspoon cinnamon	1 egg
¼ teaspoon nutmeg	1 cup milk
	¾ cup chopped raw apple

Sift flour with baking powder, salt, cinnamon, and nutmeg.

Cream shortening and peanut butter with sugar, beating until light and fluffy. Add egg and beat well. Stir in milk and chopped apples. Add flour mixture and stir just enough to moisten dry ingredients.

Fill greased muffin tins two-thirds full. Sprinkle top of muffin batter with an additional 2 tablespoons sugar mixed with a quarter teaspoon cinnamon. Bake in a hot oven (400°) 20–25 minutes.

Yield: 15–18 2-inch muffins

PEANUT BUTTER CINNAMON ROLLS

ROLLS:

¾ cup milk	1 package active dry yeast
2 tablespoons margarine	
⅓ cup mashed potatoes	¼ cup warm (not hot) water
½ teaspoon salt	
3 tablespoons sugar	1 egg
½ cup peanut butter	3 cups sifted flour (about)

Scald milk. Add margarine, potatoes, salt, sugar, and peanut butter, mixing to blend. Cool. Add yeast to water and stir until dissolved. Add with egg to milk mixture. Add 1 cup of flour and beat about 1 minute. Gradually add as much more flour as can be easily beaten into dough (about 1½ cups). Turn dough out on floured board, knead until smooth and satiny, using additional flour as needed. Place in greased bowl, brush top with melted butter. Cover. Let rise in warm place until double in bulk. Roll on lightly floured board to a rectangle 9×16¼ inches thick.

FILLING:

¼ cup softened margarine
⅔ cup sugar
½ teaspoon cinnamon

Cream margarine, sugar, and cinnamon, spread on dough. Roll as for jelly roll, beginning at wider side. Cut into quarter-inch slices. Place close together in greased 9-inch square pan.

Brush tops with melted butter. Cover, let rise in warm place until doubled in bulk. Bake in hot oven (400°) about 20–25 minutes or until crusty and browned.

Yield: 16 rolls

EASY PEANUT BUTTER PANCAKES

1 cup pancake mix   *3 tablespoons peanut*
1 cup milk   *butter*
1 egg

Combine all ingredients and beat until smooth. Bake on a preheated, lightly greased skillet or grill.

Yield: 2 servings

PEANUT CINNAMON TOAST

½ cup peanut butter 1 tablespoon margarine
½ cup dark brown sugar ½ teaspoon cinnamon

Blend ingredients until smooth. Spread on bread and toast in oven until bottom of bread is brown.

PEANUT BUTTER BISCUITS

2 cups sifted flour 2 tablespoons shortening
¾ teaspoon salt ¼ cup smooth peanut
2½ teaspoons baking butter
powder ¾ cup milk (about)

Sift dry ingredients together. Cut in shortening and peanut butter until mixture is like coarse corn meal. Add the milk and stir until a soft dough is formed.

Roll or pat on floured board to half-inch thickness. Cut with 1-inch round biscuit cutter and place on ungreased baking sheet. Bake in hot oven (450°) 10–12 minutes.

Yield: 40 biscuits

COFFEECAKE

CAKE:

2 cups sifted flour ¼ cup shortening
3 teaspoons baking 1 egg, well beaten
powder ¾ cup milk
1 teaspoon salt
2 tablespoons granulated
sugar

Sift dry ingredients together into bowl. With pastry blender or 2 knives cut in shortening until mixture resembles coarse corn meal. Combine egg and milk and add to flour mixture, stirring only enough to form soft dough. Spread mixture in greased baking pan 8×8×2 inches.

TOPPING:

½ cup peanut butter
¾ cup brown sugar, firmly packed

1 teaspoon cinnamon
2 tablespoons cream

Blend together ingredients and spread evenly on coffeecake. Bake in moderate oven (350°) 30–35 minutes. Serve warm.

Yield: 6–8 servings

QUICK PEANUT BUTTER COFFEE RING

2 tablespoons peanut butter
2 tablespoons jelly or jam

1 tablespoon milk
1 package refrigerated unbaked raisin cinnamon rolls

Combine peanut butter, jelly, and milk. Separate rolls and spread one side of each roll generously with peanut butter mixture. On a lightly greased cookie sheet slightly overlap rolls, spread side up, to form a circle. Press rolls together lightly where they overlap. Bake in a preheated (375°) oven for about 20 minutes. Frost with icing that is included in package. Serve hot.

Cakes and Pies

DATE CHEESECAKE

¼ cup peanut butter
¼ cup butter, softened
1¾ cups finely crushed
   graham cracker crumbs
1½ cups chopped dates
1 cup sugar
4 eggs, slightly beaten

2 8-ounce packages
   cream cheese, softened
1 cup smooth peanut
   butter
2 teaspoons vanilla
¼ teaspoon salt

Combine the ¼ cup peanut butter with butter and blend with cracker crumbs. Press mixture on bottom and sides of well-buttered 9-inch spring-form pan. Arrange chopped dates on bottom crust. Gradually add sugar to eggs, beating until mixture is thick and lemon-colored. Add cream cheese, a small portion at a time, beating well after each addition until mixture is smooth. Blend in the 1 cup peanut butter, vanilla, and salt. Pour filling over dates and bake in moderate oven (350°) for about 45 minutes, until cake is set in center. Allow to stand on cooling rack at room temperature for a few hours, and then refrigerate before applying topping.

TOPPING:

½ pint dairy sour cream
1 tablespoon sugar
1 teaspoon orange rind

Blend sour cream, sugar, and orange rind. Spread on cake and bake in a very hot oven (475°) for about 5 minutes. Garnish with halved dates if desired. Cool before cutting.

Yield: 12 servings

SPICE CUPCAKES

½ cup peanut butter
½ cup butter
1½ cups brown sugar,
  firmly packed
2 eggs
2 cups sifted flour
3 teaspoons baking
  powder

½ teaspoon salt
½ teaspoon ground
  cloves
½ teaspoon cinnamon
1 cup milk
1 teaspoon vanilla

Cream together peanut butter and butter. Add sugar gradually and cream together until light and fluffy. Add eggs, one at a time, beating well after each addition. Add dry ingredients, which have been sifted together, alternately with combined milk and vanilla, beginning and ending with dry ingredients. Spoon batter into greased and floured cupcake pans (or use paper bake cups to line pans). Bake in moderate oven (350°) for about 25 minutes. Cool and frost.

Yield: 2 dozen medium-sized cupcakes

LAYER CAKE

½ cup smooth peanut
  butter
¼ cup butter
1½ cups brown sugar,
  firmly packed
2 eggs
2 cups sifted cake flour

2 teaspoons baking
  powder
½ teaspoon soda
1 teaspoon salt
⅔ cup milk
1 teaspoon vanilla

Cream together peanut butter and butter. Add brown sugar gradually and cream together until light and fluffy. Add eggs and beat well. Add dry ingredients, which have been sifted together, alternately with combined milk and vanilla, beginning and ending with dry ingredients. Beat well after each addition. Pour batter into 2 greased and floured 8-inch pans. Bake in moderate oven (350°) for about 30 minutes.

Yield: 6–8 servings

PEANUT BUTTER PICNIC CAKE

2½ cups sifted cake flour
2 teaspoons baking powder
½ teaspoon baking soda
1 teaspoon salt
½ teaspoon cinnamon
¼ teaspoon allspice
1½ cups sugar
½ cup shortening, softened
½ cup smooth peanut butter
¾ cup milk
2 eggs
1 teaspoon vanilla
1 loaf-size package milk chocolate frosting mix

Sift flour with baking powder, baking soda, salt, cinnamon, allspice, and sugar. Beat the shortening and peanut butter until creamy and blended. Add sifted dry ingredients and milk. Stir to blend. Then beat 2 minutes on electric mixer or 300 strokes by hand. Add eggs and vanilla. Beat 1 minute more (150 strokes by hand). Grease and flour an 8-inch square baking pan. Bake at (350°) for 60 minutes. Cool thoroughly. Frost top with chocolate frosting, prepared as directed.

Yield: 16 servings

PEANUT ORANGE LUNCH BOX CAKE

2 cups sifted flour	2 eggs
1 teaspoon soda	1 cup reconstituted
½ teaspoon salt	frozen orange juice
½ cup peanut butter	1 cup dairy sour cream
¼ cup butter or	1 cup raisins, finely
margarine	chopped
1½ cups sugar	¼ cup dates, finely
1 teaspoon grated	chopped
orange peel	2 tablespoons honey

Sift flour with soda and salt. Cream peanut butter, margarine, and sugar together until light and fluffy. Beat in orange peel and eggs. Add ½ cup of the orange juice and sour cream alternately with flour mixture, stirring just enough to blend. Fold in raisins and dates. Spread batter in a well-greased and floured pan 12×9×2 inches. Bake in a moderate oven (350°) 35 minutes or until almost done. Combine remaining orange juice with honey and pour over cake. Continue baking cake 5 minutes or until done. Cool in pan. Cut in squares.   *Yield:* 24 pieces

APPLE PEANUT CAKE

¼ cup butter or	1 teaspoon baking soda
margarine	1 teaspoon salt
½ cup peanut butter	½ teaspoon cinnamon
1 cup sugar	¼ teaspoon nutmeg
1 egg	¼ teaspoon cloves
1¼ cups sifted flour	1 cup canned applesauce

Cream together butter, peanut butter, and sugar. Add egg, beat well. Sift dry ingredients together. Add alternately with applesauce to creamed mixture. Pour into greased, wax-paper-lined pan 8×8×2 inches. Bake in a moderate oven (350°) 40 minutes or until done. Cool 5–10 minutes, remove from pan to rack. Cut into squares. Frost with QUICK CARAMEL FROSTING (given below).

Yield: 9 squares

QUICK CARAMEL FROSTING

½ cup butter
1 cup brown sugar,
  firmly packed

¼ cup milk
1¾–2 cups sifted
  confectioners' sugar

Melt butter in 8-inch skillet. Add brown sugar. Cook over low heat, stirring constantly, 2 minutes. Add milk. Stir until mixture comes to a boil. Remove from heat. Cool. Slowly add confectioners' sugar, beating well with spoon after each addition, until thick enough to spread.

Yield: fills and frosts 2 8- or 9-inch layers, or generously frosts cake 8×8×2 inches or 9×9×2 inches

PEANUT BUTTER CANDY PIE

1 unbaked 9-inch pie
  shell
3 eggs
½ cup sugar
1 cup light corn syrup
1 teaspoon vanilla
¼ teaspoon salt

½ cup smooth peanut
  butter
½ cup semisweet
  chocolate chips
¼ cup angel flake
  coconut

Make pie crust from half of a standard recipe or half of a package of crust mix. Beat eggs. Gradually beat in sugar, mixing well. Mix in corn syrup, vanilla, salt, and peanut butter, blending thoroughly. Pour into pie shell. Bake in slow oven (300°) 40–45 minutes. While pie is still hot, put a circle of chocolate chips in center and sprinkle remaining chips around outside edge. Fill in remainder of top with coconut. Cool to serve.

Yield: 6–8 servings

PEANUT BUTTER CREAM PIE

½ cup sugar
½ cup flour
¼ teaspoon salt
1½ cups milk, scalded
2 egg yolks, well beaten
½ teaspoon vanilla

½ cup peanut butter
1 cup cold milk
1 baked 9-inch pie shell
  or 8 baked 3½-inch
  tart shells

Combine thoroughly sugar, flour, and salt. Add small amount of scalded milk; stir until smooth. Add to remaining milk in double boiler and cook 15 minutes, stirring occasionally. Pour small amount over egg yolks, blend, return to double boiler and cook 2–3 minutes longer. Cool and strain. Add vanilla. Place peanut butter in bowl; add half of the cold milk, whip with rotary beater until smooth; add remaining milk, whip until smooth. Blend with cooled custard. Chill. Pour into pie shell or individual tart shells.

MERINGUE

2 egg whites
¼ cup sugar

Beat egg whites until foamy. Add sugar, 2 tablespoons at a time, beating after each addition until sugar is thoroughly blended. Continue beating until mixture will stand in peaks. Pile lightly on filling. Bake in moderate oven (350°) 15 minutes.

Yield: 8 servings

SOUR CREAM CHIFFON PIE

1 tablespoon (1 envelope) unflavored gelatin	¼ teaspoon salt
⅔ cup cold water	⅔ cup smooth peanut butter
2 eggs, separated	1 cup dairy sour cream
½ cup sugar	1 baked 9-inch pie shell

Soften gelatin in cold water. Beat egg yolks, sugar, and salt together in top of double boiler, stir in gelatin, and cook over boiling water, beating constantly with rotary beater, until mixture is thick and fluffy. Remove from heat and blend in peanut butter. Beat egg whites until stiff but not dry and fold with sour cream into gelatin mixture. Pour into pie shell and chill in refrigerator until firm. Serve topped with slightly sweetened whipped cream and shaved chocolate if desired.

Yield: 6–8 servings

NUTTY PIE CRUST

1 cup sifted flour	¼ cup peanut butter
1 tablespoon sugar	¼ cup shortening
½ teaspoon salt	2 tablespoons water

Sift flour with sugar and salt into mixing bowl. With pastry blender or 2 knives cut in peanut butter and shortening. Sprinkle water over mixture and mix with fork until dough holds together. Press into ball with hands and roll out on lightly floured pastry cloth into a circle large enough to fit a 9-inch pie pan and allow for a 1-inch overhang. Fit dough loosely into pan and make a tall fluted edge at rim of pan. Prick dough with tines of fork and bake in hot oven (425°) for about 8 minutes, until nicely browned.

Yield: 1 9-inch pie shell

GRAHAM CRACKER PIE CRUST

¼ cup peanut butter
2 cups graham cracker crumbs, finely crushed

¼ cup sugar
2 tablespoons water

Blend peanut butter into combined cracker crumbs and sugar. Add water and knead mixture gently. Press into bottom and sides of well-buttered 9-inch pie pan. Chill thoroughly and use with favorite filling.

Yield: 1 9-inch pie shell

Cookies

PEANUT BUTTER DATE COOKIES

4 cups sifted flour
1 teaspoon baking
  powder
¼ teaspoon baking soda
1 teaspoon salt
1 teaspoon cinnamon
½ teaspoon nutmeg

½ cup peanut butter
1 cup margarine
1 cup brown sugar,
  firmly packed
⅔ cup granulated sugar
2 eggs
1 cup chopped dates

Sift flour with baking powder, soda, salt, and spices. Cream peanut butter and margarine together. Gradually stir in sugars, beating until light and fluffy. Add eggs and beat well. Gradually add flour mixture, mixing to blend. Mix in dates, which have been sprinkled with 1 tablespoon additional flour. Shape into 4 rolls about 8 inches long. Wrap in plastic food wrap, waxed paper, or foil. Chill well in refrigerator. When ready to bake, cut into thin slices and bake on an ungreased baking sheet in a moderately hot oven (400°) 5–8 minutes. *Yield:* 6½ dozen cookies

Unbaked cookie dough may be stored in refrigerator for several weeks.

PEANUT BUTTER MOLASSES SQUARES

1½ cups sifted flour
½ teaspoon salt
1½ teaspoons baking
  powder
¼ teaspoon soda
1 teaspoon cinnamon
½ teaspoon cloves

⅓ cup shortening
½ cup peanut butter
½ cup sugar
½ cup unsulphured
  molasses
1 egg
½ cup hot water

Sift flour with salt, baking powder, soda, and spices. Cream shortening, peanut butter, and sugar together until light and fluffy. Blend in molasses and egg. Add flour mixture alternately with hot water, stirring only enough to blend. Turn into greased pan 13×9×2 inches. Bake in moderate oven (350°) 25 minutes. Cool and cut into 15 squares. Serve with scoop of vanilla ice cream and PEANUT BUTTER TOPPING.

Yield: 15 squares

PEANUT BUTTER CINNAMON CRINKLES

¾ cup sifted flour
1 teaspoon soda
¼ teaspoon salt
½ teaspoon cinnamon
½ cup peanut butter
¼ cup shortening

½ cup brown sugar,
  firmly packed
½ cup granulated sugar
1 egg
1 teaspoon vanilla

Sift flour with soda, salt, and cinnamon. Mix peanut butter with shortening. Add sugars and cream until light and fluffy. Beat in egg and vanilla. Stir in dry ingredients. Chill 10 minutes. "Shoot" from cookie gun onto aluminum cookie sheet, spacing cookies 2 inches apart. Bake in a moderate oven (375°) 8–10 minutes.

Yield: 5–6 dozen medium-thick cookies

PEANUT BUTTER TAFFY COOKIES

½ cup smooth peanut
  butter
½ cup shortening
¾ cup sugar
¼ cup molasses

1 egg
2½ cups sifted flour
½ teaspoon salt
3 teaspoons apple-pie
  spice

Mix peanut butter with shortening. Gradually beat in sugar, then molasses, then egg. Sift flour, salt, and spice and blend into peanut butter mixture. Roll out a little less than a quarter inch thick on floured board. Cut into desired shapes. If you care to, decorate before baking with cinnamon red hots and silver shot. Bake at (375°) for 8 minutes or until lightly browned. Cool on wire racks. After baking, cool and complete trimming with confectioners'-sugar frosting, colored sugar, and multicolored sprinkles.

Yield: 40–50 cookies

PEANUT APPLE TEA STICKS

¾ cup sifted flour
1 teaspoon baking powder
½ teaspoon cinnamon
¼ teaspoon salt
1 egg

¾ cup light brown sugar, firmly packed
¼ cup milk
1 teaspoon vanilla
½ cup peanut butter
1 cup chopped raw apples

Sift flour with baking powder, cinnamon, and salt. Beat egg until light and gradually beat in sugar. Stir in milk, vanilla, and peanut butter. Fold in flour mixture and apples. Spread in greased square pan 8×8×2 inches. Bake in moderate oven (350°) 30–35 minutes. Cool in pan for about 5 minutes. Cut into 24 finger-shaped pieces. Roll in sifted confectioners' sugar.

Yield: 24 sticks

FESTIVE PEANUT CRISPIES

½ cup sugar
½ cup light corn syrup
1 cup peanut butter
1 teaspoon vanilla
1 cup chopped peanut
    chocolate candy bars
    or peanut candy bars

2½ cups crisp rice
    cereal

Mix sugar and corn syrup together and blend in peanut butter. Add vanilla and chopped candy. Add cereal, stirring until well blended. Roll into small balls.

Yield: 2½ dozen crispies

HONOLULU COOKIES

2 cups sifted flour
1 teaspoon baking
    powder
¾ teaspoon salt
⅓ cup shortening

½ cup peanut butter
1 cup sugar
1 egg, unbeaten
1 can (8¾ ounces)
    crushed pineapple

Sift flour with baking powder and salt. Cream shortening and peanut butter with sugar until light and fluffy. Add unbeaten egg and pineapple. Stir in sifted flour mixture. Form into oblongs on cookie sheet, 1 heaping teaspoon to each cookie. Bake in moderate oven (375°) 10–12 minutes.

Yield: 4 dozen cookies

FROSTING (optional):

1½ cups confectioners'   Chocolate-covered
  sugar   peanuts
2 tablespoons hot water
1 tablespoon butter or
  margarine

Mix sugar with about 2 tablespoons hot water and 1 tablespoon butter or margarine. Put one teaspoon in the center of
each cookie and top with a chocolate-covered peanut.

PEANUT BUTTER COCONUT CRISPS

2 cups sifted flour   1 cup brown sugar,
1½ teaspoons baking   firmly packed
  powder   1 egg
¼ teaspoon salt   2 tablespoons honey
½ cup margarine   1 cup flaked coconut
½ cup peanut butter

Sift flour with baking powder and salt. Cream margarine,
peanut butter, and sugar together until light and fluffy. Beat in
egg and honey. Fold in flour mixture until just blended. Stir
in coconut. Shape into rolls about 2 inches in diameter. Wrap
in waxed paper and chill in refrigerator overnight or until
firm. Slice an eighth inch thick. Bake on an ungreased baking
sheet in a moderate oven (375°) for about 12 minutes.

Yield: 6 dozen crisps

PERSIAN PEANUT DROPS

1 cup unsifted confectioners' sugar	1 teaspoon vanilla
⅛ teaspoon salt	¾ cup peanut butter
3 egg whites, unbeaten	¾ cup chopped dates
	½ cup flaked coconut

Add sugar and salt to egg whites and stir until sugar is dissolved. Add remaining ingredients. Mix well. Drop from teaspoon on greased aluminum baking sheet. Bake in a moderate oven (350°) 15 minutes.

Yield: 3–3½ dozen cookies

PEANUT BUTTER CRISPS

1 cup soft butter or margarine	1 egg
½ cup peanut butter	1 teaspoon vanilla flavoring
½ cup granulated sugar	1⅓ cups sifted flour
½ cup brown sugar, firmly packed	1 cup corn-flake crumbs
	Spanish salted peanuts

Blend butter and peanut butter; blend in sugars. Add egg and vanilla; beat well. Stir in flour, mixing thoroughly. Shape dough into small balls; roll in corn-flake crumbs. Place on greased baking sheets. Press one peanut into each ball. Bake in moderate oven (350°) for about 15 minutes.

Yield: about 4 dozen cookies, 2 inches in diameter

MINCEMEAT PEANUT BUTTER COOKIES

4 cups sifted flour
2 teaspoons baking
powder
1½ teaspoons salt
⅔ cup shortening
1 cup peanut butter

2 cups sugar
2 eggs, unbeaten
½ cup milk
2 teaspoons vanilla
1½ cups moist
mincemeat

Sift flour with baking powder and salt. Cream shortening and peanut butter with sugar until light and fluffy. Add eggs, milk, vanilla, and mincemeat. Stir in sifted flour mixture. Form into balls on cookie sheet (about 1 teaspoon each). Bake in moderate oven (375°) 10–12 minutes.

Yield: 8 dozen cookies

PEANUT BUTTER MAPLE SLICES

2 cups sifted flour
½ teaspoon soda
½ teaspoon salt
½ teaspoon baking
powder
½ cup shortening
½ cup smooth peanut
butter

½ cup brown sugar,
firmly packed
½ cup maple or maple
blended syrup
1 egg
1 cup chopped peanuts

Sift flour, soda, salt, and baking powder together. Mix shortening and peanut butter. Add sugar, syrup, and egg, beating until light and fluffy. Blend in flour mixture. Shape dough into 2 rolls 2 inches in diameter. Roll in chopped peanuts. Wrap in waxed paper or plastic food wrap and chill several hours. Slice into thin slices. Bake on an ungreased baking sheet in a moderate oven (350°) 12–15 minutes.

Yield: 4½ dozen cookies

PEANUT BUTTER BANANA COOKIES

1½ cups sifted flour
½ teaspoon baking powder
¾ teaspoon salt
¾ teaspoon cinnamon
¼ teaspoon nutmeg
½ cup margarine

½ cup peanut butter
1 cup sugar
1 egg
1 ripe banana, mashed
1½ cups quick-cooking oatmeal

Sift flour with baking powder, salt, cinnamon, and nutmeg. Cream margarine, peanut butter, and sugar together until light and fluffy. Beat in egg and banana, fold in flour mixture and oatmeal until just blended. Drop by teaspoonfuls on greased baking sheet. Bake in moderate oven (375°) 8–10 minutes. *Yield:* 4½ dozen cookies

CHRISTMAS SWEETIES

½ cup sugar
½ cup light corn syrup
1 cup smooth peanut butter
1 teaspoon vanilla

1 cup mixed candied fruit
2½ cups honey-flavored puffed wheat

Combine sugar, corn syrup and gradually blend in peanut butter. Stir in vanilla and candied fruit, then mix in cereal, stirring until evenly distributed. Drop by teaspoonfuls or roll into small balls. Let stand on waxed paper 30 minutes before storing. *Yield:* 50 cookie-candies

NOTE: These cookie-candies can be rolled in flaked coconut, confectioners' sugar or decorated with peanuts or whole candied cherries.

CHOCOLATE PEANUT BUTTER COOKIES

1 cup peanut butter	*4 cups sifted flour*
1 cup shortening	*1 cup cocoa*
2½ cups granulated sugar	*4 teaspoons baking powder*
4 eggs	*1 teaspoon salt*
2 teaspoons vanilla	*1 cup milk*

Cream peanut butter and shortening together. Add sugar and beat until light and fluffy. Add eggs and vanilla and beat well. Sift dry ingredients together and add to creamed mixture alternately with milk, mixing only enough to blend. Drop by teaspoonfuls on ungreased cookie sheet. Bake in a moderate oven (400°) 8–10 minutes.

Yield: 7 dozen cookies

PEANUT BUTTER REFRIGERATOR COOKIES

1½ cups sifted flour	*1 cup brown sugar, firmly packed*
½ teaspoon baking soda	
½ teaspoon salt	*1 egg*
½ cup margarine	*1 teaspoon vanilla*
½ cup peanut butter	

Sift flour with soda and salt. Cream margarine, peanut butter, and sugar until light and fluffy. Beat in egg and vanilla.

Fold in flour mixture until just blended. Shape into rolls about 2 inches in diameter. Wrap in wax paper and chill in refrigerator overnight or until firm. Slice an eighth inch thick. Bake on an ungreased baking sheet in a moderate oven (375°) for about 12 minutes. *Yield:* 6 dozen cookies

PEANUT BUTTER DREAMS

PASTRY-LIKE BOTTOM LAYER:

½ cup peanut butter
¼ cup margarine
½ cup light brown
  sugar, firmly packed

1 cup sifted flour

Blend peanut butter and margarine together. Gradually beat in sugar. Work in flour with back of spoon. Pat into bottom of greased 8-inch square pan. Bake in moderate oven (350°) 15 minutes. Meanwhile make the *torte*-like topping.

TOPPING:

2 eggs, well beaten
1½ cups light brown
  sugar, firmly packed
¼ cup flour
½ teaspoon baking
  powder

¾ cup flaked coconut
1 cup (6 ounces)
  semisweet chocolate
  pieces
1 teaspoon vanilla

Beat eggs with brown sugar until creamy. Blend in flour and baking powder. Fold in remaining ingredients. Pour over prebaked mixture. Bake 30 minutes more at same temperature. Cool thoroughly in pan. Cut in squares.

Yield: 16–20 bars

CRISSCROSS COOKIES

1 cup peanut butter
½ cup butter
½ cup granulated sugar
½ cup brown sugar,
  firmly packed
½ teaspoon vanilla

1 egg
1½ cups sifted flour
¾ teaspoon soda
½ teaspoon baking
  powder
¼ teaspoon salt

Cream together peanut butter and butter. Add sugars gradually and cream together until light and fluffy. Add vanilla and egg and beat well. Stir in flour, sifted together with soda, baking powder, and salt. Mix thoroughly. Chill dough. Shape into 1-inch balls and place about 2 inches apart on cookie sheet. Flatten with a fork in crisscross pattern. Bake in a moderate oven (375°) 10–12 minutes.

Yield: 5 dozen cookies

OATMEAL REFRIGERATOR COOKIES

½ cup peanut butter
½ cup butter
2 cups brown sugar,
  firmly packed
1 teaspoon vanilla
2 eggs

1¾ cups sifted flour
2 teaspoons soda
¾ teaspoon salt
1½ cups rolled oats
½ cup chopped nuts

Cream together peanut butter and butter. Add sugar gradually and cream together until light and fluffy. Add vanilla and eggs and beat well. Mix in flour, sifted together with soda and salt. Then add rolled oats and nuts and shape dough into rolls about 2 inches in diameter. Wrap in waxed paper or plastic food wrap and chill in refrigerator. Slice ⅛ inch thick, place on cookie sheet and bake in a moderate oven (350°) for about 15 minutes.

Yield: 6–6½ dozen cookies

TWO-WAY DISCS

½ cup peanut butter
.1 cup butter
½ cup granulated sugar
½ cup brown sugar,
   firmly packed
1 egg

1 teaspoon vanilla
1½ cups sifted flour
¼ teaspoon salt
1 teaspoon cinnamon
¼ cup chopped nuts
Shredded coconut

Cream together peanut butter and butter. Add sugars gradually and cream together until light and fluffy. Beat in egg and vanilla. Mix in flour sifted together with salt. Chill dough slightly. Shape into small balls. Roll half the balls in mixture of cinnamon and nuts. Roll remaining balls in shredded coconut. Place about 2 inches apart on cookie sheet and bake in moderate oven (375°) for about 15 minutes.

Yield: 5 dozen cookies

Desserts, Sauces, and Frostings

PEANUT BUTTER ICE CREAM BALLS

1 cup graham cracker
  crumbs
¼ cup peanut butter
2 tablespoons sugar

¼ teaspoon cinnamon
1 quart vanilla ice cream
Chocolate-flavored syrup

Blend graham cracker crumbs, peanut butter, sugar, and cinnamon. Scoop ice cream into large balls and roll in crumb mixture until well coated. Freeze until serving time. Serve with chocolate syrup.

Yield: 6–8 servings

PEANUT BUTTER ICE CREAM

½ cup peanut butter
2 egg yolks, beaten
⅔ cup sugar
¼ teaspoon vanilla

Dash of salt
1 can (14½ ounces)
  evaporated milk

Add peanut butter to egg yolks and mix well. Add remaining ingredients and beat until well mixed. Pour into freezer tray. Freeze until frozen 1 inch in from edges of tray (about 1 hour). Turn into a chilled bowl. Beat until smooth. Return to freezer tray and freeze until firm (about 1½ hours).

Yield: 4–6 servings

PEANUT BUTTER RIPPLE ICE CREAM

¼ cup peanut butter
6 tablespoons honey
1 quart soft vanilla ice cream

Blend peanut butter and honey. Put half of vanilla ice cream in freezer tray. Cover with layer of peanut butter. Add remaining ice cream. With a spoon stir so that peanut butter is mixed partially with ice cream. Refreeze.

Yield: 4–6 servings

HOLIDAY PUDDING

¾ cup sifted flour
¾ teaspoon baking soda
¼ teaspoon salt
½ teaspoon nutmeg
¼ teaspoon allspice
⅛ teaspoon clove
½ cup margarine
½ cup peanut butter

1 egg, slightly beaten
⅓ cup dark corn syrup
Grated rind of 1 lemon
Juice of 1 lemon
1 cup chopped dates
1 cup shredded carrots
⅓ cup raisins
Whipped cream

Sift flour, baking soda, salt, and spices together. Cream margarine; blend in peanut butter. Beat in egg, then stir in corn syrup, lemon rind and juice. Mix in sifted dry ingredients, then dates, carrots, and raisins. Spoon into 6 greased 5-ounce custard cups. Place in pan of hot water. Bake in moderate oven (350°) until knife inserted near center of pudding comes out clean, about 55–60 minutes. Unmold and serve warm, garnished with whipped cream.

Yield: 6 servings

PEANUT BUTTER PUDDING

2 cups cold milk
½ cup crunchy peanut butter
1 3¾-ounce package instant pudding (any flavor)

Pour milk into mixing bowl. Add peanut butter and pudding mix and beat slowly just until well mixed, about 1 minute. Pour into serving dishes. Let stand to set, about 5 minutes. *Yield:* 4 servings

PEANUT BUTTER CRUMB PUDDING

½ cup peanut butter
2 cups graham cracker crumbs
½ cup light brown sugar, firmly packed
1 3¾-ounce package instant vanilla pudding

2½ cups milk
1 ⅗2 can pineapple chunks, drained
Sweetened whipped cream

Mix peanut butter, graham cracker crumbs, and sugar with fork or pastry blender until crumbly.

Prepare instant pudding as directed on package, using 2½ cups milk. When mixture is thickened, fold in drained pineapple chunks.

Butter an 8-inch square pan. Divide crumb mixture into thirds. Pat one-third into bottom of buttered pan. Carefully spoon one-half the custard over the crumbs. Pat one-third of the crumbs over this pudding layer and spoon in remaining custard. Top with remaining crumbs. Chill in refrigerator for several hours. Cut into squares or spoon into sherbet glasses. Serve with sweetened whipped cream.

Yield: 8 servings

PEANUT BUTTER JELLY PUDDING

2 cups cold milk
½ cup crunchy peanut
  butter
1 3¾-ounce package
  instant vanilla pudding
  mix

¼ cup grape jelly

Pour milk into mixing bowl. Add peanut butter and pudding mix and beat slowly just until well mixed, about 1 minute. Pour into serving dishes. Let stand to set, about 5 minutes. When ready to serve, spoon a tablespoon of grape jelly in the center of each serving. *Yield:* 4–5 servings

APPLE CRUMBLE

½ cup sifted flour
½ cup sugar
¼ cup margarine
¼ cup peanut butter
4 cooking apples

¼ cup sugar
½ teaspoon grated
  lemon rind
2 tablespoons lemon juice
2 tablespoons water

Measure flour and the ½ cup sugar into mixing bowl. Cut in margarine and peanut butter with pastry blender or 2 knives until coarse crumbs form. Pare, core, and slice apples. Arrange in 1½-quart casserole or shallow baking dish. Sprinkle with the ¼ cup sugar, lemon rind, lemon juice, and water, then cover with crumb mixture. Bake in moderate oven (350°) until apples are tender, about 45 minutes. Serve warm, topped with ice cream or whipped cream.

Yield: 6 servings

BAKED APPLES

6 medium baking apples
¼ cup peanut butter
1 cup light or dark corn
  syrup

½ cup water
½ teaspoon cinnamon

Core apples. Peel upper half. Place in shallow baking dish. Stir peanut butter and ¼ cup corn syrup together until blended. Spoon into centers of apples. Combine remaining ¾ cup corn syrup with water and cinnamon. Pour over apples. Bake in moderate oven (350°), basting frequently, until apples are tender, about 1 hour. Serve hot or cold.

Yield: 6 servings

MINIATURE GRAHAM TORTES

½ cup peanut butter
½ cup chopped dried
  apricots
½ cup shredded coconut
2 tablespoons honey
2 tablespoons orange
  juice

½ cup whipping cream
24 graham crackers
1 cup whipping cream
Candied fruit, nuts, or
  toasted coconut

Combine peanut butter with apricots, coconut, honey, and orange juice. Whip the ½ cup cream and fold into peanut butter mixture. Spread on 16 of the crackers. Stack 2 of these crackers together and top with a plain cracker. Repeat with remaining crackers. Whip the 1 cup cream and frost sides and tops of the *"tortes."* Refrigerate to let cream set and allow flavors to blend. Garnish with candied fruit, nuts, or toasted coconut.

Yield: 8 miniature *tortes*

BAKED CUSTARD

2 *cups milk*
½ *cup smooth peanut*
  butter
3 *eggs, slightly beaten*

½ *cup sugar*
¼ *teaspoon salt*
½ *teaspoon vanilla*

Blend ½ cup of the milk into peanut butter. Gradually add remaining milk, beating until smooth. Combine eggs with sugar, salt, and vanilla and blend into peanut butter-milk mixture. Pour into buttered 1-quart baking dish and bake in slow oven (325°) for about 45 minutes, until knife inserted halfway between side of baking dish and center comes out clean. Garnish with whipped cream and bits of candied fruit or bright jelly if desired.

Yield: 5–6 servings

HOT FUDGE-NUT SAUCE

1 *6-ounce package (1 cup) semisweet chocolate pieces*
1 *small can (⅔ cup) evaporated milk*
¼ *cup peanut butter*

Combine all ingredients in a small saucepan and stir over low heat until chocolate melts and mixture is smooth. Serve warm over ice cream, cake, or pudding. Sprinkle each serving with chopped peanuts. Leftover sauce can be stored in the refrigerator and reheated over low heat. Add a little more milk if sauce is too thick.

Yield: 1½ cups

MAPLE-NUT SUNDAE SAUCE

⅓ cup crunchy peanut butter
⅔ cup maple blended syrup

Mix peanut butter with syrup until mixture is smooth.
Serve over orange milk sherbet or vanilla ice cream.

Yield: 5–6 servings

PEANUT CARAMEL SAUCE

1 cup light brown sugar,
  firmly packed
1 tablespoon flour
⅛ teaspoon salt

1 cup water
½ cup peanut butter
1 teaspoon vanilla

Mix sugar, flour, and salt. Stir in water. Cook and stir
over low heat until mixture comes to a full rolling boil. Add
peanut butter and bring again to a boil, stirring constantly
to make a smooth mixture. Remove from heat. Add vanilla.
Serve hot or cold over ice cream. *Yield:* 1½ cups

MILK CHOCOLATE-
PEANUT BUTTER FROSTING

¼ cup smooth peanut
  butter
¼ cup butter
1 package milk chocolate
  frosting

¼ cup milk
½ teaspoon vanilla

Cream peanut butter and butter together with a wooden spoon or electric mixer. Add frosting mix and milk alternately, stirring until well blended. Add vanilla. Beat 1 minute or until frosting is creamy.

Yield: frosting for 2 9-inch cake layers

PEANUT BUTTER BAKED-ON FROSTING

2 egg whites	½ cup crunchy peanut
¼ teaspoon salt	butter
1 cup brown sugar	

Beat egg whites with salt until stiff. Gradually beat in brown sugar. Fold in peanut butter.

Spread on hot baked cupcakes. Return to oven and continue baking 5–7 minutes longer.

Yield: frosting for 24 large cupcakes

VELVET FROSTING

½ cup smooth peanut butter	1 teaspoon vanilla
¼ cup softened butter	3–4 tablespoons cream or milk
2½ cups sifted confectioners' sugar	

Cream together peanut butter and butter. Blend in remaining ingredients and beat until smooth. Add enough cream to make frosting of good spreading consistency.

Yield: frosting for 2 dozen cupcakes or 2 9-inch cake layers

"SWIRL" FROSTING

1½ cups sugar
2 egg whites
2 teaspoons light corn
    syrup

Dash of salt
⅓ cup water
1 teaspoon vanilla
¼ cup peanut butter

Mix together sugar, egg whites, corn syrup, salt, and water in top of double boiler. Place over boiling water and cook, beating continuously, until frosting is light and fluffy and holds in stiff peaks when beater is withdrawn (about 6–7 minutes). Beat in vanilla. Frost cake, reserving about ¼ cup of frosting to blend with the peanut butter for "swirls" on top and sides. Use about a teaspoon of the mixture for each swirl, placing it in the frosting and "swirling" with the tip of the spoon.

Yield: frosting for 2 9-inch layers

PEANUT BUTTER TOPPING

½ cup sugar
½ cup flour
½ teaspoon salt

3 tablespoons peanut
    butter
3 tablespoons shortening

Combine sugar, flour, and salt in small mixing bowl. Cut in peanut butter and shortening until crumbly.

Yield: topping for 1 9-inch pie

Confections

PEANUT PENUCHE

2 cups brown sugar,
  firmly packed
Dash of salt
1 tablespoon light corn
  syrup

1 cup milk
½ cup peanut butter
1 teaspoon vanilla

Combine sugar, salt, corn syrup, and milk in heavy sauce-pan. Cook, stirring only until sugar is dissolved, to soft-ball stage (236° on a candy thermometer). Cool, without stir-ring, until lukewarm (110°). Blend in peanut butter and va-nilla and beat until mixture holds shape. Spread in buttered 8-inch pan. Cool and cut.

Yield: 20–24 pieces

DOUBLE PEANUT CLUSTERS

½ cup peanut butter
1 cup semisweet chocolate or butterscotch bits
1 cup whole salted peanuts

Combine peanut butter and chocolate or butterscotch pieces in top of double boiler and place over hot (not boiling) water until chocolate or butterscotch melts. Stir until blended. Add peanuts and stir until well coated. Drop by teaspoonfuls onto waxed paper-lined baking sheet. Chill until set.

Yield: 2 dozen clusters

PEANUT COCONUT JEWELS

1 cup peanut butter
½ cup honey
1 cup California
  seedless raisins

1 teaspoon vanilla
1–1½ cups angel flake
  coconut

Mix peanut butter with honey, raisins, and vanilla. Spread coconut on waxed paper or flat pan. Drop spoonfuls of peanut mixture on coconut and roll to coat completely with coconut. Chill.

Yield: about 3 dozen candies

EASY PEANUT BUTTER
CHOCOLATE FUDGE

1¼ cups sugar
¼ cup peanut butter
½ cup evaporated milk
1 cup marshmallow fluff

½ teaspoon salt
1 cup (6-ounce package)
  semisweet chocolate bits

Combine sugar, peanut butter, milk, fluff, and salt in saucepan. Cook and stir over low heat until blended. Continue cooking and stirring until mixture comes to a full boil. Boil 5 minutes, stirring constantly.

Remove from heat. Add chocolate. Stir until chocolate is melted and blended into cooked mixture. Pour into greased pan 8×8×2 inches. Cool. Cut into squares.

Yield: 36 pieces

APRICOT CANDY ROLL

3 cups granulated sugar
½ cup peanut butter
1 cup milk
1 cup chopped or
　ground dried apricots

½ teaspoon salt
2 teaspoons vanilla

Combine sugar, peanut butter, milk, apricots, and salt in saucepan and stir over moderate heat until well mixed. Cook without stirring to 238° (small amount dropped in cold water forms soft ball). Remove from heat. Cool until outside of pan feels cool. Add vanilla. Beat until creamy and easy to handle. Then turn out on buttered platter and work with hands until very smooth and satiny. Shape into 2 long rolls. Chill at least 3 hours and slice thin.

Yield: 2 pounds of candy

DOUBLE DECKER
PEANUT BUTTER FUDGE

2 cups sugar
2 tablespoons light corn
　syrup
¼ teaspoon salt
¾ cup milk
1 square unsweetened
　chocolate, cut in small
　pieces

1 teaspoon butter
3 tablespoons peanut
　butter
1 teaspoon vanilla

Combine sugar, corn syrup, salt, and milk in saucepan. Place over medium heat and stir constantly until sugar is dissolved and mixture boils. Cover tightly and cook 2 minutes. Uncover and continue cooking, without stirring, to 232° (small amount dropped in cold water forms soft ball). Remove from heat. Place chocolate and butter in second saucepan and carefully pour in half of the hot syrup. Cool both mixtures to lukewarm (110°) without stirring. To plain mixture add peanut butter and ½ teaspoon vanilla. Beat until mixture is thick and has lost its gloss. Pour at once in buttered pan 8×5 inches. Add ½ teaspoon vanilla to chocolate mixture. Beat until mixture is thick and has lost its gloss. Spread over first layer. When cold cut in 1-inch squares.

Yield: 40 pieces

POPCORN PEANUT EASTER EGG

1 package ready-to-pop corn	1 square unsweetened chocolate
1 cup light corn syrup	Pressurized cake frosting
1 cup sugar	
¼ teaspoon salt	
½ cup crunchy peanut butter	

Butter a 1½-quart melon mold well. Pop popcorn in its own foil fry pan according to directions on lid. Mix corn syrup, sugar, salt, peanut butter, and chocolate together in a 3-quart saucepan. Place over medium heat, stirring constantly, until sugar dissolves and chocolate melts. Add popped corn and stir until all corn is coated. Continue cooking, stirring constantly, until popcorn kernels begin to stick together. Press into buttered mold. Let stand until cold. Then unmold. Decorate as Easter egg with pressurized cake-frosting decorator. Slice and serve with ice cream.

PATIO PEANUT BUTTER FUDGE

2 cups sugar
3 tablespoons butter
1 cup evaporated milk
1 cup crunchy peanut
butter

1 cup miniature
marshmallows
1 teaspoon vanilla extract
2 squares unsweetened
chocolate

In an electric skillet combine sugar, butter, and evaporated milk. Set control for 300°. Bring mixture to a boil. Boil about 5 minutes, stirring constantly. Turn off heat. Add peanut butter, marshmallows, vanilla, and chocolate. Stir until all ingredients are melted and blended. Pour into a buttered 8-inch square pan. Cool and cut into 1-inch squares.

Yield: 5 dozen

PEANUT BUTTER CRINKLES

5 cups puffed rice cereal
5 cups crisp rice cereal
½ cup butter

1 pound marshmallows
(cut up)
½ cup peanut butter

Grease a large bowl with butter. Put cereals in bowl and stir to mix. Combine butter, marshmallows, and peanut butter in the top of a double boiler. Cook and stir over boiling water until marshmallows are melted and blended. Add to cereals and stir until mixed with mixture. Pack into 2 greased 8-inch square pans. Cool and cut into squares.

Yield: 32 squares

PEANUT BUTTER MARSHMALLOW FUDGE

1 cup light brown sugar, firmly packed
1 cup granulated sugar
¼ teaspoon salt
½ cup milk

1 cup bite-size marshmallows
½ cup peanut butter
1 teaspoon vanilla

Combine sugars, salt, and milk in saucepan. Cook until mixture forms a soft ball in cold water (240°). Remove from heat and add marshmallows, peanut butter, and vanilla. Beat until thick and creamy. Pour into buttered pan 8×8×2 inches. Cool. When firm cut into 1-inch squares.

Yield: 5 dozen

PEANUT BUTTER FUDGE

⅔ cup milk
2 cups granulated sugar
1 cup marshmallow fluff
1 cup crunchy peanut butter

1 teaspoon vanilla
½ cup chopped dates

Combine milk and sugar in saucepan. Boil without stirring to 240° (soft ball forms when a little is dropped in cold water). Remove from heat. Add marshmallow fluff, peanut butter, vanilla, and dates. Stir only until combined. Pour into greased pan 8 inches square. Place in refrigerator at least 20 minutes before cutting. Cut into 1-inch squares.

Yield: 5 dozen

A POSTSCRIPT FOR BIRD WATCHERS

Peanut butter, of course, is made for people. But there is no denying the fact that for years bird lovers across the nation have also dipped into the peanut butter jar on behalf of their feathered friends.

In bird feeding many people spread a thin layer of peanut butter on the trunk or stuff it into holes and crevices of a tree. Others serve it mixed with seed in grapefruit halves that have been scooped out. Some ornithologists suggest, as a formula for bird feeding, approximately three-fourths of a container of seed to one-fourth of a container of peanut butter.

Mr. Duryea Morton, director of the Audubon Center at Greenwich, Connecticut, and a member of the permanent staff of the National Audubon Society, has been feeding peanut butter to his birds for years. Mr. Morton utilizes hanging sticks into which holes have been drilled as containers for peanut butter. Such diverse containers as coconut shells and clamshells have also been used successfully for bird feeding, but Mr. Morton stresses that the important factor is the accessibility of the container rather than its shape or size. His reply to those who decry the use of wire feeders, in the belief that they may be injurious to the eyes of the birds in cold weather, is that in his experience birds will always maneuver themselves into eating position with care.

Peanut butter is over 26 per cent pure protein, and birds get more than adequate supplies of this precious element when peanut butter is added to their diet.

The beauty of feeding peanut butter to birds is that your variety of dinner guests is almost unlimited. What birds will you find staying for dinner? That depends a good deal on where you live, but the birds known to enjoy its smooth, nutty flavor are woodpeckers, jays, and chickadees, as well as robins, flickers, juncos, thrushes, nuthatches, brown creepers, and the curve-billed thrashers.

It is doubtful if bird fanciers really ponder the gustatory pleasures that birds derive from their food, but they do know that food tossed from a kitchen window or served in a feeder may save their lives. The birds, in turn, reward their benefactors by filling the summer gardens with song and the empty winter window sills with friendship.

Index

INDEX

MORE COOKBOOKS, REFERENCE AND HUMOR FROM BART

☐ 002-X MOVIE GUIDE FOR VCR's by The Philadelphia $5.95
    Inquirer   Canada $6.95
☐ 007-0 DAY CARE PARENTING by April Hubbard & $3.50
    Clementine Hayburn   Canada $4.50
☐ 024-0 THE 500 CLUB: BASEBALLS GREATEST SLUGGERS $2.95
    by The Philadelphia Daily News   Canada $3.95
☐ 052-6 CONDOMANIA: 101 USES FOR A CONDOM $5.95
    by Peter Maddocks   Canada $6.95
☐ 025-9 THE CHOCOLATE COOKBOOK by William $3.50
I. Kaufman   Canada $4.50
☐ 026-7 THE 'I LOVE PEANUT BUTTER' COOKBOOK $3.50
    by William I. Kaufman   Canada $3.95
☐ 036-4 THE CRAB BOOK by Cy and Pat Liberman $3.95
                                           Canada $4.95
☐ 038-0 WALK DON'T DIE by Fred A. Stutman, M.D. $3.95
                                           Canada $4.95

Buy them at your local bookstore or use this handy coupon:
Clip and mail this page with your order
_____

BART BOOKS
Dept. MO
155 E. 34th Street, 12E
New York, NY 10016

Please send me the book(s) I have checked above. I am enclosing
$_____ (please add $1.00 for the first book and 50¢ for each
additional book to cover postage and handling). Send check or money
order only—no cash or C.O.D.'s.

Mr./Mrs./Ms _____
Address _____
City _____ State/Zip _____
Please allow six weeks for delivery. Prices subject to change without
notice.